———— LIVE FROM ————

CUPERTINO

——— LIVE FROM ———
CUPERTINO

How Apple Used Words, Music, and Performance to Build the World's Best Sales Machine

michael hageloh
with Tim Vandehey

Post Hill
PRESS

A POST HILL PRESS BOOK
ISBN: 978-1-64293-170-9
ISBN (eBook): 978-1-64293-171-6

Live from Cupertino:
How Apple Used Words, Music, and Performance to Build the World's
Best Sales Machine
© 2019 by Michael Hageloh with Tim Vandehey
All Rights Reserved

Cover art by Ryan Allen Vincent
Interior design and layout by Sarah Heneghan

Post Hill Press
New York • Nashville
posthillpress.com

Published in the United States of America

To Lisa, one day in 1988, I answered a call on my Motorola DynaTAC (with car kit and quarter wave external antennae) and accepted a position with a crazy little small market share company called Apple Computer. It was destiny and the beginning of a unique journey. Still hidden from me that day was the greater life journey that would be revealed just twelve months later when I got married. Today, though I'm still a diamond in the rough, I'm fortunate to share my life with a beautifully polished gem who, thirty years later, is still with me—unlike the DynaTAC, which thankfully came and went.

I owe you my life. You insisted that I get that small spot checked and saved me from a deadly melanoma—and you pushed me when I wanted to quit writing this book.

Without you, this book would never have happened, and so consider it yours. Though it can never live up to the love I have for you, it is unquestionably a tribute to it.

Thank you for the past, and let's get going with the future.

I love you

TABLE OF CONTENTS

What Were Once Devices Are Now Habits

When I set out to write this book, one of my goals was to see if I could insult fifty million people in one sentence. Here goes. Years ago, before I was excommunicated from New York City and became a resident of Texas (a state so unusual that someone in our town once asked my wife and me if being Jewish was like being Catholic), I lived in Florida, which is so appealing to the unbalanced that when I took the "Florida Challenge" (where you google "Florida man" and your birthday to see what kind of headlines pop up) for April 24, the first result read, "Florida man kisses venomous snake and is immediately bitten on the lips."

Mission accomplished. Now, let's move on.

While living in the Meme State, I went to Orlando to attend a conference, and while there I tried to crash a speech by a guy named Daniel Smith, who had written a book called *How to Think Like Steve Jobs*. Security was tight, and I couldn't charm my way in with my stories about a monkey and some mayonnaise. But the room was packed. Who was this guy, and what insights about Jobs might he bring to the table?

Well, I shouldn't have bothered. I did a little research, and it turned out Mr. Smith had written more than ten books on the "How to think" theme, about icons ranging from Bill Gates to Leonardo da Vinci—people he obviously hadn't met any more than he'd met

Steve. His main qualification seemed to be that he'd been an Apple *customer* for eight years. Based on that logic, I'm qualified both to practice internal medicine and run a Jewish deli. So come on down to Michael Hageloh's Primary Care and Pastrami, where you can get medication to lower your cholesterol followed by a meal to raise it!

Still, there was that auditorium and its wall-to-wall attendees. That's the power of the Steve Jobs myth and the Apple brand. Ever since "Think Different," the world has ached to know how Apple did it. What was the secret sauce? How did Apple create the Cult of Mac and become the world's first trillion-dollar corporation? Then there's the question every entrepreneur, designer, and would-be startup CEO wants the answer to:

How can I be more like Steve Jobs?

You can't. Sorry. There was only one Steve. How do I know? Because I worked for Apple from 1988 to 2010, making my exit not long before Steve made his own exit due to pancreatic cancer. I worked with Steve's most lauded customer: educators. I wasn't in the garage when he and Woz cobbled together the Apple I in 1976, so I didn't see everything, but I saw *almost* everything:

- The sad "beige box" days when we forgot who we were and tried to be who everybody else thought we should be;
- The March of the Generic CEOs;
- The near-death of the company, when we were nearly sold to archrival Microsoft;
- Our thrilling turnaround in 1997 after Steve resumed his role as leader;
- The spectacular rebirth—led by the iPod and iTunes—that would one day make Apple the world's most valuable corporation.

Am I a designer? An engineer? One of Steve's right hand men? No. Again, sorry to disappoint you. I'm nowhere near that interesting. For most of my time at Apple, I was part of the company's Higher Education sales, the line of business that kept the company alive during the dark years. I spent my days calling on colleges and universities all over the country, trying to persuade their departments—from music to physics to athletics to colleges of business—that Apple products would take their students into the twenty-first century. And I guess I did something right, because I closed nearly $1 billion in deals before I packed up my dollies to try my luck with Adobe and a handful of startups.

Wait a sec, go back. Apple has enterprise-level salespeople (aka account executives)? Don't its products, well, sort of...sell themselves?

Yes, it does. But I don't blame you for thinking that. After all, that's what CEO Gil Amelio told us at our annual sales meeting in 1997, when the company was weeks from acquisition or bankruptcy. He said, "Get out of the way. These things sell themselves." You can imagine how dandy that was for our morale. It's also dead wrong.

If you're in sales or know anything about sales, you know that no product, no matter how wonderful, sells itself. Second, even products as brilliant and world-changing as the iPhone face headwinds. There are entrenched systems, concerns about things like price points and sales channels, and the fact that truly new and different products scare the bejesus out of some people. Products don't sell themselves. Salespeople do that.

Still, the first part of my tenure at Apple was tough. Our creative mojo left with Steve, and Macs were a tough sell. "No one ever gets fired for buying IBM," went the conventional wisdom. We were on life support through most of the '90s. I went home many Fridays wondering if I would have a job on Monday. But I was the only one in my territory who was never laid off, and it was because I didn't push boxes. I sold myself first, Apple second, and the product third. I practiced the truest version of selling: building relationships based on trust and finding the creative moments that led to one record-breaking deal after another.

But you've heard all that before. You've read sales books about relationship-building and customer relationship management (CRM). You've trained on all the systems at seminars that bored you into a coma. Good thing I'm not here to talk about that stuff. I'm here to share the sales story that no one's ever shared publicly—to walk you behind the scenes of the most iconic, obsessed-over brand in the history of consumer products and answer the question every sales professional wants to know: "How did Apple do it?"

In a word, it was *music.* Musicality was in the DNA of nearly everyone who worked at One Infinite Loop in Cupertino, California, in those days. In the '80s and again in the late '90s and 2000s, music suffused Apple's culture. You thought it was a coincidence that it was the iPod and iTunes that brought the company back from the brink? Our employees were musicians, performers, composers, producers, creative rebels, and entertainers. That's one reason journalist Umair Haque, blogging for the *Harvard Business Review*, wrote, "Apple is less like a company. It's more like a band. It makes stuff it loves. It doesn't care what you think. Not you, critic, nor you, competitor, nor me, analyst, nor you, loyal Apple fan. Not a single one of us. It cares whether what it makes is good by its own standards—good enough to love."

That's right, and that same love and passion for music didn't stop at design and engineering. It carried over to us in sales. Because selling is more like performing live than any other part of business. It's just you and the audience in real time, with you trying to make a connection and inspire them to join you on a journey. You're reading the room, improvising and working without a net, and when you can bring real fire and joy to the performance, you're at your best. That's when you love selling, and the customer loves you right back.

Steve Jobs was part poet, part lead singer; part dictatorial producer screaming orders from the booth. We were at our best when he was at the front of the room like an orchestral conductor, and when he left the company, he took the music with him. From 1985-1997, Apple was elevator music, Auto-Tune, easy listening—bland and inoffensive. That nearly killed the company.

When Steve came back, he instantly revived our dormant musicality and the company with it. That made "Think Different," the iMac, iPod, iPhone, and iPad not only possible, but made them products that changed the world—products everyone had to have. To put it another way (and to borrow from the title of a great Doobie Brothers record), what were once devices were now habits.

But in some ways, those amazing products were a *harder* sell than the old desktop computers because the unfamiliar requires persuasion. Our job was to make Steve's vision tangible for people who'd never met him or heard him make his presentations. Turnkey sales techniques—the IBM method, the Xerox method, the Herman Miller method—weren't going to get it done.

Technology wasn't much help, either. *Salesforce.com* can give you the facts and figures, but it can't sense hidden opportunities. It can't demonstrate emotional intelligence. It can't dazzle. Apple didn't even have a corporate Customer Relationship Management (CRM) system until 2006, and when we finally got one, we wrote it in-house. I know, because I was one of many test humans. Today, Apple Retail has turned that CRM into a competitive advantage.

So how the hell did we do it?

The methodology was that there was no methodology. I suppose it would be more accurate to say that our methodology was about who we were, not what we did. If you're looking for a successful sales methodology, start by asking your top people. They already know what it is because they're using it. Importing a methodology from outside will just waste time and money and alienate those same stars.

That doesn't mean Apple didn't try to buy sales success. We did. We bought a number of external methodologies from vendors. One was called "Hope is Not a Strategy," and it lasted a few months. Others fizzled even faster. The engine that not only made Apple sales rattle and hum (apologies to U2) but shaped our legendary culture was our passion for music and our penchant for weaving its elements—rhythm, harmony, storytelling, and so on—

into every department and everything we did. That's why Apple was such a great fit for me.

Who am I? Oh yeah, we'd better spend a little time on that part of the story.

—✦—

I was born in Tampa, Florida, the child of two immigrants: one from Germany and one from Hungary. Neither spoke English when they immigrated. My mother emigrated from Germany at sixteen and worked in food service in the Hillsborough County Public Schools for much of my life, so education was always a priority in our small family. I know little about my father, as he passed away when I was two. He was involved in union organizing work for the longshoremen, which is why my parents moved to Tampa—to be near the docks. Apparently, he also wrestled under the name "Lucky Louie." Mother never spoke much of him except to say (with her classic sharp wit), "Your father said he knew what he was doing, and now look." I'm not sure I was a planned pregnancy.

I ended up having the most diverse childhood imaginable, going to schools in Tampa's Cuban community, then to a mostly black school, and finally, even though we were not Catholic, to a private Jesuit high school (where I learned about, among other things, the rhetorical principle of *Eloquentia Perfecta*, which will come into play later). It was the perfect upbringing for a future musician, because I was always hearing different rhythms and learning about different cultures.

(Mother's early years were spent working at Wright's Deli on the Upper West Side of Manhattan. She earned more tips than anyone because she loved people and their stories. Her philosophy was, "I know what I know; I want to know what you know." Customers would come in for their morning coffee and say, "Where's Hanna?" I'm sure that's where I picked up my love for talking to people.)

I started playing music on a used Hammond B-3 organ; Jon Lord of Deep Purple was my idol. However, I wasn't much of a keyboardist, so I turned to percussion instead. I picked up the drums as a kid and, by the time I was a teenager, I was playing in bands and my high school marching band (I was the Oreo center—the white drummer with black drummers to either side of me). My first paying gig came when I was seventeen at the Ritz Theater in Tampa's Ybor City neighborhood. This was before Ybor became a tourist attraction; back then, it was strip-bar sketchy, and the Ritz was a dive. But a mystery man named Pepe (that's what the locals called him) gave me a break and paid me fifty dollars, which was promptly taken from me to cover a dinner of black beans and rice at the Columbia Restaurant. I spent much of the evening playing David Rose's "The Stripper," which gets into your head like "Let It Go" from *Frozen*. I loved it.

When I turned eighteen and had to fill out my Selective Service form, it was a moment I'll never forget. It struck me that life could change on a dime; at any moment, you could be called for service and never come back. I realized that I had to do something with my life, and I wanted that life to revolve around music.

So I played every kind of gig you can imagine: parties, dances, clubs; you name it. I played disco, funk, and rock and roll. I took studio work. I did everything I could to survive as a professional musician. That also meant taking a job at a radio station, playing music in a 9:00 p.m.–2:00 a.m. slot that I'm sure had an audience of about six people. But I loved it—at least, initially. Radio's a natural for me; I have that self-deprecating Jewish sense of humor and the gift of gab. Plus, I got to record a lot of the commercials myself and made a $200 talent fee per spot, which was great. Of course, the station charged $500 for my work, which was good prep for life as a musician.

But I grew to dislike my radio job. It wasn't long before I was ready to blow my brains out if I had to play "YMCA" one more time. (Side note: I saw the Village People in a small bar in Miami before they got big, and they closed with "YMCA." I remarked that it was the worst song I'd ever heard. Karma is a bitch.) I hated sitting alone in a four-foot-by-four-foot booth and talking to the less-than-sane people otherwise known as "callers." I wanted to be playing music for a live audience, feeding off their energy, not playing other people's tunes.

Then I got this thing called a Macintosh, which let you edit your own audio files. At that time, we were still editing commercials and promotions on tape, but this software called Pro Tools was a miracle. I learned it and started reworking commercials, making them more musical. That was fun! Of course, my program director—my joy-killing nemesis—said, "We're here to sell ad time, not to make ads better."

That was the beginning of the end. I was fired on a technicality, which was fine with me. Along with gigging and radio, I'd been doing roadie work because I was comfortable with technology. I was in the green room at Tampa Stadium one night in 1988, picked up a *Wall Street Journal*, and saw a classified ad from Apple Computer, Inc. They wanted to hire a Systems Engineer, someone who knew this beta product called Pro Tools and could talk about computers. That was me, so I applied. Apple hired me for the East Coast region based out of the Tampa regional office, and I thought I would be in a recording studio.

Nope. Instead, I would be the tech support for two account executives in Higher Education—a tall, great-looking guy named Ray and a guy who looked like Barney Rubble from *The Flintstones,* Craig. They were a terrific team because Ray was brilliant at opening doors, and Craig was great with the technology. Both were master salespeople. On my first day, I was handed a cassette of music called the "Apple Boogie," and my musical journey began.

Our first sales call illustrates so much of what I want to talk about. We met with the provost of the University of Florida in Gainesville—a huge potential customer. He was out of his office when we got there, but there on his desk was the Mac II demo machine. It had a card in it that would let you connect it to an IBM-based 3270 network, the standard at the time. Ironically, that 3270 card, which was part of Apple's strategy to "fit in" with the computer companies building bland beige boxes, nearly killed us. But

on that sales call, it introduced me to two critical ideas that would help Apple become Apple.

I unplugged the provost's PC and plugged the 3270 cable into the Mac II. Instantly, it was on the network. Then the provost came back into his office, saw me behind his grand desk, and saw the Mac II humming away on the network. He said, "How did this happen?"

With the glib arrogance of youth, I said, "It's magic."

I don't remember if we made a sale that day, and it's not important. What is important is the idea of *magic* and its companion, *nuance*. In those days, instantly connecting to a network was magic, because no one else did it. Apple always paid attention to nuance, the small details that, when you add them up, make magic. Steve knew that tiny improvements and unique experiences are what take you from great to superior—from "Hey, it works," to "Holy shit, that's like magic."

During those early days at Apple, Ray (Ray-Jay) introduced me to the power of music and magic in sales. People loved to talk to Ray because he was well-versed, glib, and charismatic. I never once heard him ask for the sale, because he didn't have to. One of the things that helped him bring that charisma to each meeting was his love of music.

One time, when we were on the road, I walked into Ray's hotel room and found him sitting on the edge of his bed, eyes closed, listening to the music pouring out of his Sony CD player and speakers. He listened with his entire body, swaying and lost in the rhythm and melody.

I said, "Ray, we have a meeting." Without opening his eyes, he said, "I know, I'm prepping." After a while he got up, turned the music off, went to the presentation, and killed it. His music took him to a different place, and he brought that energy to his selling. Nobody ever walked out of one of Ray's presentations saying he'd just given them specs and prices. They walked out wanting more. He was a master at asking the right questions and showing the customer that he cared. Much of what I used at Apple, I learned from him.

When I joined Apple's Higher Education sales, in my first sales meeting, they handed out little books written and signed by musician Jackson Browne. The book was called *100 Things to Get*, and one of the one hundred was, "Buy yourself a Macintosh." Musicians loved us because we were all about personal passion and creativity. Passion, creativity, nuance, magic—they were why I was able to close Apple's biggest education sale at the time, to Saint Leo University in Florida, a private Catholic school of about one thousand students. Every student got a computer. It was the first big deal of many.

_~\|/~_

I'm going to show you how I did it—how *Apple* did it. I'm the first person to write about Apple from an inside sales perspective. But I'm not just going to tell you how we sold Apple. I'm going to explain why music was so vital to our culture and our sales success, as well as how you can capture some of that magic for yourself as an individual contributor or a leader running an organization. To do that, I've stretched the musical metaphor as far as it can go, and then some.

The process of going from sitting inside an office in Cupertino to being out in the field, putting on a show for a customer, is the same as the process of bringing music from the rehearsal room to a live stage. In my first draft of this book, I focused only on rhythm because sales has a rhythm of its own. But then I realized that everything that makes live music great—words, voice, harmony, soul—was also there when Apple was at its best. A great salesperson has the same instincts as a great performer of live music: disciplined rehearsal, improvisational skill, staying ahead of the beat, telling a compelling story, and more.

I'm going to take you through each of the musical properties that made Apple sales so extraordinary, step by step, from the garage to the live stage:

- Rehearsal
- Storytelling
- Listening
- Words
- Rhythm
- Improvisation
- Soul
- Orchestration
- Magic

I'll explain how each of those aspects of musical expression came to fruition in Apple's sales and culture. More importantly, I'll deconstruct them so you can understand how to find the music in your sales process and or organizational culture. I'll lay out how and why implementing musicality in your sales is different if you're a manager or an individual contributor. I'll also share a lot of stories and examples about how we did what we did at Apple—and yes, plenty of stories about Mr. Jobs.

I'm also going to toggle back and forth between speaking to the individual sales professional and the VP of sales or sales manager running a sales department. Some of my advice will be useful for both, while some of it will only make sense for individual reps or management. I trust you'll figure out which is which. In any case, I think most of the information will be useful for both types of readers, even if it's not addressed to you.

What I won't do is give you Michael's Seven Easy Steps to Being a Multi-Million-Dollar Sales anything, because there aren't any. This isn't going to be as easy as that. What we did wasn't about steps and process. It was about heart, wonder, and our determination to take people where they didn't know they wanted to go and astonish them when they arrived. So don't expect just-add-water steps or systems. What I'm going to tell you, you've got to *feel* in your bones and your gut like a beat.

Not everybody can do that. You'll have to leave behind nearly everything you ever learned about selling. But if you've read this far, you're probably up for that. So enough of my backstory. Let's start. I'll count us in.

—Michael Hageloh
April 2019

CHAPTER 1

Rehearsal

noun

*re·hears·al | \ ri-'hər-səl *

A private performance or practice session preparatory to a public appearance

Examples:

David Gilmour of Pink Floyd, Prince and the Revolution, Steely Dan

It's an old groaner of a joke. A tourist in New York asks a guy, "Hey, buddy, how do you get to Carnegie Hall?"

The other guy says, "Practice, practice, practice."

The thing is, nobody's sure where the line came from. I checked with the *New York Times,* and all they know is that nobody knows. It might've been Arthur Rubinstein. It could've been violinist Jascha Heifetz. More than likely, it's one of those lines handed down in Yiddish from somebody's *bubbe.* It reached the ears of a reporter and wound up in the *New Yorker.* It doesn't matter who said it anyway. What matters is that it's true.

We live in an era that rewards speed. Launch and learn. High-speed prototyping. New businesses ramp up in weeks thanks to cheap cloud computing and minimum viable products, or MVPs.

It's easy to forget that in the race to be first to market, preparation matters. I spent twenty-two years at Apple, and when we were at our best, nothing was rushed. Nothing was left to chance. We had deadlines to hit to get new products to market, especially after Steve Jobs came back and everyone loved us again, but we only released products into the wild after months—*years*—of endless, obsessive repetition.

That's what allowed the iPod and iPhone to be so amazing. It wasn't just design and development talent, and it wasn't magic. It was work. It was *rehearsal.*

Rehearsal is the tedious repetition that turns focused attention into muscle memory and, eventually, artistry. If you're a musician, or if you've ever acted on stage, you know what I mean. I spent years drumming in live shows with rock and roll and funk bands, and almost as much time in the studio laying down tracks for commercials. I know that the early iterations of any tune, when you first try to get the tempo and insert the right rolls and fills, are tedious and frustrating. You start and stop, start and stop, mess up and begin again. That's the process. In the studio, it wasn't unusual for us to do ten takes until we were ready to murder the engineer.

But that's what it takes to get to greatness. Again, think back to a school or community play. Even if you weren't one of the stars, you probably remember the difference between the lead actor's performance before he memorized his lines and after he had them down cold. It's the same for an athletic activity like hitting a baseball or swinging a golf club. When you have to focus all your conscious attention on getting the details right, you're just a machine repeating the same actions.

When you master the details and can do them automatically, you can internalize the beat, the notes, the lines and blocking of the play, or the mechanics of swinging a two-iron and make them your own. The action slows down and you can start to bring nuance and subtlety to what you're doing. You stop being a robot and start being an artist.

The ability to do that only happens as a result of tedious, tiresome, let's-go-through-it-for-the-seventeenth-time rehearsal. I spent thousands of hours (from lessons, to my high school band, to my disco days) in home studios, practice spaces, and garages, fine-tuning rhythms, attacks, breaks, fills, riffs, and performance skills. It was fun, but it was definitely work. But that's how sound and rhythm become music. If you're a musician, tattoo this on your arm (or some other body part):

> *Quality of a band's performance = Time spent in rehearsal.*

I bring all this up because music infused everything that Apple did. Our first blockbuster mobile product of the post-exile Jobs era—the one that started Apple's evolution from a computer company to a world-shaping innovator—was a music player: the iPod. Remember it? You might not, because the iPhone has eclipsed it. But back in 2001, when the iPod debuted, the idea of a sleek MP3 player with a simple navigational scheme that could hold *one thousand songs* was nothing short of revolutionary. When you added iTunes, which had debuted eight months earlier, it was Mind. Blown.

Now, think back to those iconic iPod ads from the early-to-mid 2000s, the ones with young people rocking out in silhouette to color-saturated backgrounds. That's what music was to Apple when I was there: pure joy. Pure passion. *Love.* That's why I connected so perfectly with the company and why I could sell its products so well.

In the music industry, people use a different kind of language than in corporate America. It's not about faster-better-cheaper. It's the language of heart, of what feels right. Apple understood, instinctively or because of Steve's remarkable instincts, the difference between its products and so many others: *nobody needed them to survive.* Nobody *needs* an iPhone, iPad, or Apple Watch. You might *want* those things, but your kids aren't going to starve if you don't have them. Music is the same way. You can love music (or art, or film, or baseball) down to your bones, but you won't die if you can't consume it. In order for you to want to buy it and pay a lot of money for it, you have to love it. *Crave it.*

Apple understood that. Everything we did, from our designs to the language we used with customers, was built to touch the heart. We didn't lead with features and benefits because we knew our customers wanted to feel the passion the dancers in those iPod commercials felt. After all, when was the last time you swooned to a love song where the singer wailed, "Baby, please come back because I like your shoes and you know the Netflix password..."?

Music is about heart. Apple was, too. So our sales had to be.

A few words on...practice:

Rehearsal and practice are different things. Practice is something you can do in the privacy of your home, standing in front of a mirror. It's detached from the circumstances. Rehearsal happens in a group, with everyone taking cues from everyone else. You're an ensemble, synched up in harmony. In selling, rehearsal happens when you're working with other salespeople, simulating the sales situation, maybe even under the kind of pressure we were while we waited for Jobs to call on one of us to strut our stuff. You should do both, but rehearsal is more important, because it helps you learn to think on your feet. You don't learn to play "I Feel Good" sitting at home. Remember, pressure makes diamonds.

Obsessive Attention to Every Detail

We brought out that heart through rehearsal and disciplined preparation. Not just in product design but in the relationships we built with our customers in sales. With any band, the product that gets people dancing or makes them cry begins in the rehearsal room. It's the same with any company.

Taking time to "get it right" was critical in sales because pre-Steve, nobody in the corporate world was buying Apple products. The thirty-five of us in Higher Education were the lifeblood of the company. We had to bring our A-game; it was a matter of life or death. We had to be the best of the best, so we rehearsed. We were calling on people with PhDs—literally the smartest people in any room—and in some cases, with tenure, they were permanently employed. This is an important distinction between educators and the typical customer, because tenure gave these educators absolute job security, so trying Apple products was no risk. But on the flip side, our business relationships could span years, and everything we ever promised was remembered. We had to know our stuff. We had to be *perfect.*

The only path to that level of excellence was rehearsal—by paying attention to all the small things that the big boys in the C-suite wouldn't because they thought these things sold themselves. We knew better, and when Steve came back that became especially true because Steve controlled *everything*. I'm talking the fall of every sparrow.

Prior to his return, we were all freewheeling because there was no single vision of what the company was. We made it up as we went along. The moment Steve came back, that ended. He literally dismantled our marketing team and put them into a room with curtains that nobody could see through. Then he drove them like sled dogs: *This is the new message; this is the way it's going to be done.* When we finally went out into the field to meet with customers, we could add our own pace, flair, and nuance to the presentation, but the message itself was dictated from on high, and we had rehearsed it down to the words, commas, and pauses. In musical terms, there was a score for every player to follow, and God help you if you changed one note or rest.

It helped that at Apple we had terrific copywriters, designers, and production people. Our presentations were the best of the best. We didn't have the field account executive tooling around in his Ford Taurus, throwing together something just before he met with the customer. Our presentations came down from the powers that be, and we didn't dare change a punctuation mark. You could argue that it was restrictive and that it quashed the creativity of the sales team, but have you seen Apple's market cap lately? From a sales standpoint, it *worked* better than anything that came before. Still does.

The Illusion of Effortlessness

Ceaseless work can make music or selling look easy, but you can't let yourself believe the lie that it *is* easy. It's not. When I joined Apple in 1988, the company was less than nine years old, ramping up its field sales team and expanding into the academic marketplace. At the time, there were regional offices throughout the country—Tampa, Ft. Lauderdale (a stone's throw from Boca Raton, the birthplace of the PC), Dallas, you name it—but everybody operated independently. I hopped a plane to Tennessee, interviewed with a newly minted "technical manager" there, followed up with a meeting out in California, and got the job.

I didn't have a personal sales strategy or belief system established at some other corporation. I was a musician who liked tinkering. But I bought into the vision, the individualism, and the sense of destiny long before Apple bought into *me*. When the people in charge said we were going to change the world, I believed it. I was dedicated to making that dream a reality.

While I was busy mixing and then drinking the Kool-Aid, it was not an ideal time in Apple's history. Steve had just been ousted and left to start NeXT. New management had taken over, and while they were preaching the gospel that the world was moving towards a focus on innovation, Steve wasn't the one preaching it. There wasn't a glittering *personal* vision standing front and center at the company, guiding everything. It was sort of an "every man for himself" environment that seemed cool—until you tried to get something important done. When I switched to sales, I saw that wasn't going to work. Not if I and my fellows wanted to close deals and bring in the revenue that was keeping us alive, at any rate.

We needed to be conscious about what we were doing, to plan and polish every step. There's a myth that too much preparation takes away a performer's ability to be spontaneous and invent something marvelous in the moment, and it's complete hogwash. It's a rationale concocted by people too lazy to put in the work. Successful bands rehearse until their fingers bleed. I've done it. If you haven't seen the movie *Whiplash*, watch it. Watch how Miles Teller's character, Andrew, practices the drums until his hands literally bleed. That's what it takes to be great (though I'm not claiming to be a great musician).

Endless rehearsal lets you put the essential elements of your sales performance on autopilot so you don't have to think about them. You can perform and relate and connect without saying to yourself, "Now, what was I supposed to say next?"

Try something. Take something you're really good at—typing, bowling, playing piano, whatever. Now, when you do that something, it's effortless. You don't think about it; you just do it, probably because you've been doing it for decades. But the next time you do it, make yourself think through every step. If you're typing and you use the hunt-and-peck method like most of us do, put your hands in the technically correct position you learned in school. Keep your fingers curved just so and your wrists elevated. Now, only use the proper fingers to strike each key.

Torture, isn't it? You're slow and inaccurate, right? That's because you're thinking.

Thinking too much makes smooth, natural, automatic activity stilted and awkward. What's worse, because you're using all your mental RAM to think through your swing or chords or sales pitch, you've got nothing left to be creative or adapt on the fly. Rehearsal and practice don't rob you of spontaneity; they *enable* it by freeing you to improvise, be creative, and listen. You can pay attention to body language, switch tactics on a dime, bring in nuance, rely on your instincts, and be yourself.

The best bands rehearse every week because they know that only when they have every chord, entrance, and turnaround nailed will they feel free to solo and improvise—to be musicians. Preparation is the foundation that lets you customize as you build. A salesperson for an organization that I won't name once eagerly told me that he had landed a meeting with the Chief Academic Officer of one of the top ten universities in the U.S. That is comparable to a screenwriter getting an audience with Steven Spielberg. If you're not exhaustively prepared, it's also a wasted opportunity.

I asked him what he was planning to talk about, and he started yammering on about a presentation where he would talk about ROI. Just like he always did to every other type of customer. Resisting the urge to grab him and shake him, I kept my cool and asked why he was going to lead with ROI when public universities don't track return on investment the way a big corporation might, because they're funded by public funds, research grants, and foundation dollars.

Blink-blink. He had no answer.

So I shot him.

I'm kidding. But my trigger finger was really itchy.

Rote selling is a guaranteed failure in the education market, in small business, in the corporate world...really in *any* market, because we live in a world where a customer can go online and find the best price for an item and all its technical specs in the time it takes to heat water for tea.

Sales teams that approach everything and everyone the same way are like an American walking through Paris and talking in slow, loud English to the locals. They assume that because they speak this language, everyone else should *parlez-vous Anglais* too. They aren't trying to understand the people on the other side of the table. Instead, they're thinking about getting from point A to point B, focused only on what is important to them, watching their map without looking up to see if everyone is still following along. Most of the time, they're not.

An Annoying Musical Interlude

In 1970, the Doors were set to record their album *L.A. Woman*, which would be their last with Jim Morrison as lead singer. But they didn't record it at a studio owned by their label, Elektra Records. Instead, wanting their own space, they set up a rehearsal space and recording studio in an old antique store on Santa Monica Boulevard in West Hollywood, California. There wasn't a sonically isolated vocal booth for Morrison to lay down his vocal tracks, so he sang in the bathroom, taking advantage of the natural reverb.

The lesson: Make your rehearsal conditions and process your own. Do what works for you and your team and brings out the best in each of you.

Will You Be Ready When the Spotlight Lands On You?

Intense, constant creative brainstorming, planning, and the endless design and messaging iterations for which Steve became infamous were the secret sauce that helped Apple—and my sales department—achieve that brand of quasi-effortless excellence. Everything became intentional; nothing was haphazard or accidental.

When Steve came back to lead the company in 1997, he became the symbol and chief practitioner of the obsessive, neurotic preparation that became our hallmark. For example, it was well known inside the company that he spent days—sometimes a week or more—practicing every nuance of his presentations for his audiences, our annual developers conference, and the sales teams.

How many executives do that? If you were ever fortunate enough to see any of Steve's presentations live or online, every single detail—no matter how trivial—had been rehearsed to the point of exasperation. He left nothing to chance even though it might have looked casual and unplanned. He drove technical crews insane with his attention to even the most mundane details, but it was for a good reason.

Interesting side note: When Steve visited with the Education Sales division, he gave a very Spartan presentation. Just two stools and some water, without a single slide. In musical terms, Steve was playing *a capella*—without instrumental accompaniment. Why? I have a theory. This was the leader of the band at his simplest. Without the bells and whistles, it was just Steve making a direct connection to those who would carry his message forward. It was brilliant.

Steve and I shared a philosophy: rehearsal doesn't just mean that you're prepared for a specific event in advance. It also means being ready with knowledge, insights, and strategies so if you're surprised, you can land on your feet. For example, in every sales meeting that I attended, every person who was customer-facing had to be ready to make an off-the-cuff presentation to our peers, senior leadership, and possibly even Steve himself. The trick was, we didn't know which one of us the spotlight would impale like a bug on a pin.

So we all sat there sweating, hundreds of education salespeople, praying we wouldn't be put on the spot. It was like being back in middle school math class when you hadn't done the homework and prayed the teacher wouldn't call on you. Finally, leadership would tap someone to get up and "sell." Steve might be in the room, but you didn't know. For all you knew, you were selling for your job. (If you're an aficionado of *RuPaul's Drag Race*, this was the sales version of "Lip Sync for Your Life.") At the end, you got a grade. If it wasn't a good grade...well, you'd better hope it was, or you'd better have an updated résumé.

Stressful? You bet. But try performing for your real audience when you're unprepared. That's one hundred times more stressful, because it's all on the line. If you can thrive under those conditions, when the pressure to perform is on, then you're either in sales, a musician, or both.

How to Sharpen a Knife with a Butterfly

Steve and my musical career taught me that anyone who wants to stay on top—a band, a theatre troupe, a corporation—has to keep improving and pushing the boundaries of what's possible. You do that through practice and rehearsal. Nobody walks on-stage improvising, unless that's what they planned on doing...and even improvisation has rules and methods. In sales and musical performance, you're always looking for tiny inflection points that can give you an edge. How do you get on stage? How will you exit? Where is the light? Where's the acoustical sweet spot?

One of the most enjoyable tours of 2019 was the "Pray for the Wicked" tour by Panic! At the Disco. One of the things that made it so much fun was the performance of front man and lead singer Brendon Urie, and that performance usually kicked off with a stunning entrance. In most venues, instead of just walking on-stage, Urie was *launched onto the stage through a trapdoor by a hidden trampoline.* Yep. You think that took a wee bit of staging and practice?

Selling is a show; have you rehearsed? Have you at least looked over what you're going to say? I'll ask that of young salespeople at the startups I still consult for, and they'll wave me off and say, "Michael, I've made this pitch a hundred times. I've got this." That's exactly when you make the mistake that kills you. That's exactly when you stumble. Happens every time.

Being a master at sales means you're always rehearsing so you can be automatic and instinctive. It means never assuming you know your pitch cold no matter how many times you've done it. Great musicians and performers, from Yo-Yo Ma to Eric Clapton, still rehearse every day. That's how you go from great to superior!

You should always be pushing yourself, because you only have two options:

1. *Get a little better each time you get in front of a customer.*
2. *Become complacent and lose your edge.*

There's no middle ground. You can't run in place and get ahead. Sales is a dynamic profession; you're either growing and developing or losing ground to the competition. I live by that rule today, and when I was at Apple, it was my guiding star.

I always had butterflies in my stomach when I got in front of the customer. It didn't matter how well I knew the product or how many times I'd rehearsed what I was going to say. Even today, when I speak to groups about this book or talk to the team at a startup, even when I'm getting ready to say things I know like the back of my hand, I get jittery.

I welcomed those butterflies, and I still do. Why? They keep me—well, I was going to say *humble*, but I'm really not very good at humility. Just ask my wife, Lisa. No, the jitters prevent me from becoming complacent—or worse, self-congratulatory. They remind me that I can always screw up. So I'm always putting pressure on myself to make my presentation better. I'm always selling, even if today I'm selling myself and my knowledge, not products.

You're always selling, whether you're selling a product, a service, your ideas, or yourself. You can always be more prepared, more knowledgeable, more rehearsed. There's no such thing as too professional.

Three Kinds of Rehearsal

But what do I mean by rehearsal? Are we talking about just sitting in a room going over scripts and pitches? Absolutely not. There are three types of rehearsal that any sales team needs to make a habit:

> 1. **Technical rehearsal**—At Apple, our sales training wasn't "Five easy things to learn and deliver." It was about emotion and communication. But that started with going over the technology again and again and again so that we knew every aspect of how these devices were designed and built, how they worked, and what they could do. Add the artful delivery of the message—the song—and you had something powerful.

Every person on your team should possess an encyclopedic knowledge of what you're selling. They should be able to take it apart and put it back together while telling a story without missing a beat. A great band is made up of virtuoso musicians who have *chops*: first-rate technical musicianship. Everybody on the team should be an expert. That's where rehearsal begins.

2.   **Situational rehearsal**—This is about knowing everything about how you're going to approach the encounter with the customer. What are you going to talk about? Be so well prepared that it's unconscious, so you're free to riff off of what the customer says or anything that inspires you in the moment.

This also means knowing your audience down to the finest detail. The Internet lets you prepare in ways you never could before. Build a dossier on everyone who might be in the room during a sales call. If you're going for the deal of a century, scope out personal details on everyone who might be involved. Invest the time to learn who they are, what they care about, what they fear, what their problems are. How can you be their hero? Go over the information so you don't miss nuances.

Apple might have been all about music, creativity, and teaching the world to sing like it was in a Coke commercial (google that too), but in sales we were incredibly structured. When it came to knowing the audience and the presentation, "good enough" wasn't. I knew that the small details that come from research could be the difference between getting what you want and being just another rep. This still works, by the way. Recently, I was talking to a woman about a project, and I'd done my homework on her, so I said, "What a great profile you have. Cornell and then on to Columbia."

She was surprised and delighted. "Wow, you read up on me."

I said, "Absolutely. You wouldn't want to talk to me if I hadn't done my homework, would you?"

"Nobody's ever said that to me." Boom. *Instant* rapport. That, ladies and gentlemen, is how it's done. That's how I got Lisa to say yes, and she hasn't figured it out yet—I mean, we're still blissfully happy all these years later.

My suggestion? Walk through every step of your encounter, from before the beginning to after the end:

    a. Who will be in the room and their professional backgrounds

    b. Personal information—spouses, birthdays, hobbies, favorite sports teams

    c. Company information—how they did in Q3, feared competitors

    d. What materials you'll bring and where you'll carry them

    e. How you'll enter the room and start the meeting

    f. Your presentation—Do things work? Do you have backups?

    g. How will you respond to critical questions?

    h. How can you bring value to this unique group of people?

    i. Who's the decision maker, and what's the decision-making process?

    j. How will you close the encounter and exit the room?

    k. How will you follow up?

3. **"Oh, crap!" rehearsal**—No matter how well you prep, things will go sideways. People are unpredictable. Equip-

ment breaks. Once upon a time, my band played a large high school dance, and to create a dramatic effect, we set up concussion mortars and flash pots behind my drum kit. But the powder was expensive, so we didn't test the pyrotechnics beforehand. Yes, you can see what's coming, but quit smirking.

We hit the big drum roll in the Commodores' "Brick House," and right on cue the flash pots ignited behind me—and so did my shirt! Gunpowder was everywhere: in the Roland drum machine, in my hair, everywhere. We all scrambled to get somewhere that wasn't on fire, and the commotion left the audience in chaos. We were never invited back. If we'd held a brief rehearsal to make sure the effects went off the right way, things would have gone differently...and I would not have been on fire.

The "Oh crap" rehearsal helps you keep your cool when the shit hits the fan. Because it will. In person, customers will throw you curveballs. When you're prepped and the curve comes, you're not swinging from the heels and missing, then stammering and looking like an idiot. Because you've practiced for this. Rehearsal gives you safe spaces to go when the projector breaks or the customer asks you a crazy question. You stay cool and think, *Well, I know that Bob got burned by his last vendor, and he's feeling stressed, so let's address his concern openly.* And you save it.

(Let me just say for the record that if you walk into a sales meeting without the correct dongle to connect your device to the projector, it should be grounds for immediate dismissal. There are standards to be upheld, for God's sake.)

What could go wrong? Make a list. Include the likely and the unlikely. For each possible "Oh, crap!" moment, how will you or your team recover so you don't lose the meeting and the customer? When I was playing a gig or in the studio, I always had extra drumsticks at hand because I could count on losing my grip on a sweaty stick at least once a show. Guitarists keep extra strings and picks close by. Stuff happens. What backups do you need? Spare batteries, paper handouts, or a second cell phone in case yours dies? Pros don't assume things will go well. Neither should you.

Do you have a small TUMI bag with dongles? How about an Ethernet cable so you can physically connect to a network instead of relying on what could turn out to be sketchy WiFi? Once, when a substantial deal was on the table, I actually threw down one thousand dollars out of pocket for a dedicated connection in my hotel. The result: a $9 million sale. That's how we do that.

Expect the best, prepare for the worst, and hope for something in the middle.

A few words on...repetition

The defining trait of rehearsal is doing something over and over until you get it right. But "getting it right" is a little more complex that it seems. Repetition becomes the key to rehearsal when you're trying something new that makes each iteration different and, hopefully, better. Sometimes, that means hating the person running the show. It means long hours and suffering. It means what you thought was good enough wasn't. What I can promise you is that with each repetition, you'll sharpen your perceptions and get better at spotting weaknesses and fixing them before anyone else even notices them.

What You Need to Rehearse

A Common Vision—You can't have every member of a band playing their own style of music. The drummer can't be playing a blues shuffle while the lead guitar is playing an Eddie Van Halen riff and the guy on the Hammond B3 keyboard is throwing down some funk chords. You need one goal—one idea that everyone's on board with.

A sales team or a company needs a single vision coming from the top. Without it, you won't stay on message, and that can cause problems in two ways. First, they'll ricochet from one approach to another. I saw this when I was at Adobe. The company was desperate to stay on message, but there were no core values driving sales and marketing. One week, we were a creative company. The next, we were a services company. We were selling to the desktop, then we were software as a service (SaaS). We were going to sell institutional licenses on campuses—unless we sold them to individuals. It was a mess. There was no show, so why even rehearse? This led me to a profound realization:

When you don't know what kind of company you are, neither will the customer.

Nobody buys from an unknown quantity.

The other danger is that without a guiding principle, your sales team will revert to mechanical, features-and-benefits selling with no heart or storytelling. That didn't work well back when I was at Apple, and it's the kiss of death today. Today, in the age of streaming entertainment and on-demand, door-to-door everything, customers feel they're entitled to a personalized world...and they're right. If your sales or marketing team can't give them a show that feels organic and spontaneous while being structured, precise, and goal focused, they'll find someone else who can. And there is *always* someone else.

A Dedicated Space—Every group has its cherished rehearsal space. It's comfortable, secure, and has what they need to get the job done. It's like that clubhouse you had when you were a kid.

You and your sales team need the same thing. But I'm not talking about a physical space; that could be a conference room. I mean a *safe* space where everyone can speak freely, float crazy ideas, and screw up without judgment. If you don't have a space like that, find one.

The Freedom to Improvise—I think I attended about twenty-eight sales trainings in my career, and the only one I remember and still use came from an improvisational theater group. It was a lot of fun, and one of the key things I learned is that professional improv actors don't just walk out on stage and start pretending to be stuck on a building ledge. They train in proven techniques, like "Just say 'Yes, and...'" They have a big toolkit they can work with.

Rehearsal is the time to try out new techniques, stories, and sales strategies. The rule in rehearsal is "there are no bad ideas or dumb questions." Bad outcomes and stupid answers, sure. I've produced my share of both, but I digress. The point is, anything's worth trying, because you don't always know what will work. Even if ninety percent of your improvised ideas wind up on the rehearsal room floor, the two or three that work are worth it.

Bandmates You Know and Trust—Trust might be the most important outcome of rehearsal time. Live performance is a trust fall done in front of thousands of strangers. When I break my drumbeat, I have to trust that you'll be there to pick me up with your guitar fill. Otherwise, I'm sitting there with my, ahem, stick in my hand. We all have to trust that the singer knows the lyrics, the sax player will come back home after a solo, and that we'll all end a song together.

Here's what I mean. When Steve came back to Apple, we began the transition in name and in culture from Apple Computer to Apple, Inc.—from a company focused on pushing gray boxes to a company once again passionately obsessed with changing the world.

Shortly after Steve was installed as "iCEO," the entire field sales team was summoned to Cupertino for "the meeting." We knew that Apple products lacked vision; we were just hocking a different version of the same old, same old. For the love of God, we even had a Windows add-in board for the Mac II! We'd gritted our teeth through years of dealing with executives who were deaf and blind to our insights—the people who were actually in contact with the customers. We hadn't turned out a winning product in years. We'd had years of managers, not leaders.

Steve got up to speak. "We know from a product standpoint, we have not delivered," he said. We sat up straighter. This wasn't C-suite spin. It was a breath of fresh air. Because he was willing to be honest with us—to let us know that he saw what we saw—our "insanely great" culture returned almost overnight. It had been hibernating, and all it took was a leader speaking the plain truth. Suddenly, we were ready to climb mountains again.

Steve marked the return of *leadership* to Apple. By cutting through the corporate bullshit, owning what was happening, confirming what we already knew but no one had said, and turning us loose to be who we knew we could be, he earned our trust. That let us trust ourselves and each other to go out and sell the way we wanted to: putting the relationship first.

To paraphrase one of the greatest American musicals of all time, *The Blues Brothers*, Steve "put the band back together."

Rehearsal lets the members of a band know and trust each other. Being in the same room for months, with no glamour or audience—just amps, craft beer (one of the benefits of age is that you start drinking better beer), and work—builds the relationship that every band has to have in order to create great music. At Apple, we led with relationships inside and outside of the organization. There was mutual respect between sales and marketing, sales and product, sales and hardware engineering, and sales and software. For the first time, sales was included in everything.

That was unusual. It still is. More often, a company's salespeople are put in an enclosure like zoo animals, while everyone else walks by and points.

"Look, son, those are our salespeople down there. Aren't they ugly?"

"Daddy, what are we?"

"We're 'corporate,' son. Eat your cotton candy, and we'll go look at the giraffes."

The key to building trust is time spent together working and solving problems, and we had that. As we refocused on selling the relationship with our customers, we also refocused on our relationships with each other and with Apple's departments. People stopped spending all their time on the road because they were pissed off. We spent time in the rehearsal space working on chord changes and tempos. A great band or team comes into being during those times when everyone is getting their hands dirty.

If your sales aren't what they should be, ask yourself: how much time does your team spend in rehearsal versus being on the road, on their devices, in meetings, or on their devices in meetings?

The Road to the Stage—Manager

At this early point, you and your bandmates should be finding your rehearsal groove: locating the right safe space, setting a schedule, figuring out what your repertoire will be, figuring out who's responsible for the equipment and, of course, deciding who brings snacks. It's not exaggerating to say that any group's successes or failures start at rehearsal. Now is the time to make regular collaboration, brainstorming, and obsessive attention to detail part of your organization's sales culture.

The Road to the Stage—Individual Contributor

You might have a band to work with, but even if you don't, you can and should rehearse on your own. Become a student of the music—the emotional appeal of what you're selling and the value you're providing. Of course, this is also the time to become technically proficient, playing scales or singing lines until your eyes burn or your throat gets sore. If you don't have an ensemble to collaborate with, establish your own rehearsal routine—that time and place where you do research, weave stories, and develop your plans for when things go sideways. The thing is, when your sales colleagues see the results of your rehearsal, they'll almost certainly ask you how you did it. Then you'll have a band.

Don't Pitch; Know and Adapt

Finally, don't waste time rehearsing your pitch. People don't want to be pitched. They want to be inspired. That's what made Apple so amazing after Steve took over. We started inspiring each other again, so we inspired our customers. They could sense our joy and passion. Everything in the startup world is pitch, pitch, pitch. It becomes robotic.

At Apple, if you relied on a memorized pitch, you were dead meat. Example: at every sales team meeting, somebody had to present and sell to the rest of us. It was a ritual. The leader would point to somebody and say, "Give me a presentation for a regional district summit." That person had to give an impromptu presentation, and if it was a national sales meeting, the entire national team got to critique them. Talk about tough. But that's how you get to great, then to superior.

Did that happen to yours truly? You bet it did. Once, we had a worldwide sales meeting in California. The entire global education sales team (more than three hundred people) was in the room. We had been talking about the new version of our Final Cut Pro editing software. Our vice president, Barry Wright, walks by, points to me, and says, "Hageloh. You want to convert a film school from analog to digital with Final Cut. I'm the dean of the film school. Tell me about it."

I stood and took the mic. Speaking to Barry like he was the film school dean, I said, "I could take the four-million-dollar editing lab that you just installed and transition that to every tree on campus."

He looked at me and said, "What do you mean?"

I said, "Because now with the power of the MacBook and Final Cut on the individual device, you have a studio in every student's hand, *anywhere*, under any tree on campus. Would that improve the program?" A big grin broke out on Barry's face. I'd nailed it. I didn't always, but it sure felt good when I did. And in fact, I did convert one of the first film schools in the country, at Florida State University, to non-linear editing on Final Cut, despite a faculty set in its traditional analog ways.

That was the outcome of hours and hours of rehearsal. I had been thinking about college conversion. I wasn't going to hit my $39 million number one dollar at a time. I had to do something big. Final Cut had become a big product. The idea of turning a room-based lab into a portable editing suite and taking it into the real world was a new concept. But I knew it was compelling. So I planned. I thought it through. I rehearsed. When I got in front of my university audiences, I knew their decision making process. I was free to take them on journey from inside the classroom to sitting under a sycamore tree, editing a film. I had them in the palm of my hand.

I don't believe in the pitch. Wean yourself off yours now. Relying on a pitch makes you inflexible. I believe in preparation, rehearsal, knowledge, storytelling, and then trusting your instincts depending on how the show is going. That's how you read the room and relate to the audience. You can speed up or slow down. Adapt to the moment. That's why, when people ask me, "What's your elevator pitch?" I reply, "It depends on who's in the elevator."

Rehearsing empowers you to sell based on *context*. To sell to a dean at the University of Florida, I had to know him personally, but I also had to understand his context. Was he a dean who wanted to take his college to a new place? A comfort dean? A management-only dean? A true academic? Knowing the context of the situation you're walking into is like knowing the room before your band sets up to play. Will you be seated at a round table where everybody is relatively equal, or a long table with the leader at the head?

Ignoring context and setting is like being a drummer and ignoring the stage. You don't know where to set up or where the audience is. You leave your performance to chance. You lose your advantage. Great sales is showmanship. Quit clutching a pitch, specs, or a sales system like you're Linus with his blanket. Do your homework. Practice. Have a depth of knowledge so you can know what to say as the situation changes. If the elevator opens and the people on it aren't who you expected, you'll be ready to engage your audience, tell a story, and take them on a journey with your products waiting at the end.

Michael's Excruciating Rehearsal To-Do List:

- **Get the band together.** Be in the same place at regular times. Not on FaceTime, not on a conference call. In person. Synergistic stuff happens when smart people spend time together brainstorming and trying things out. Make it a habit.

- **Set goals, then create systems.** What are your numbers for the month, the quarter, the year? Know where you're trying to go and then figure out how to get there step-by-step. Build a repeatable system.

- **Go deep.** Start learning about your customers as people, not just as companies. Yes, learn about the company—origins, market, competitors, weaknesses, you name it. But also learn about the people in depth. Keep files on everyone, and update them regularly. Create calendar items to remind you of birthdays, wedding anniversaries, work anniversaries, etc. Make customer relationship management (CRM) tools work for you, not the other way around.

- **Become experts.** Everyone on your team needs to be a walking database on your products. Sure, each person might have a specialty—something they sell more often that they become ultra-educated about. However, it's everyone's job to be strong on all your products, services, and solutions—how they're made, how they're administered, how they're serviced, what they can do,

what they can't, pricing, sourcing, technical specs, everything from A to Z. This is sweat equity time. Study.

- **Be Batman.** Batman's superpower is that he's always thinking five steps ahead. Be Batman. Map out what could go wrong and why, and have Plans A, B, and C.

- **Put each other on the spot.** When you have so much knowledge that your skulls hurt, start challenging each other. Run scenarios, tell stories, critique each other. Remember, great selling is about trust and relationships—and that doesn't only mean relationships with your customers. It means that you and your sales team hold each other accountable, have each other's backs, and make each other better. Rehearse, become storytellers, and get to the point where improvising and adapting becomes a reflex, like breathing. Then you're ready to put on a show.

CHAPTER 2

Storytelling

noun

\ *'stôrē,teliNG* \

The telling or writing of stories

Examples:

Bob Dylan, Johnny Cash, Michael Jackson, Muddy Waters

I'll never forget talking to a friend, a very sophisticated technology guy who was loved by Apple, about the first iPod. He and I were sitting together one day, and he looked at me and said, "Who wants to carry two thousand songs in their pocket?" Seems ridiculous today, but he and many others had to be brought along on the idea of the iPod. They had to be sold on it. That was what Steve was so brilliant at doing.

He was as much a public salesperson of Apple as an internal salesman who got everybody motivated. Steve wasn't a technologist or an engineer or a designer. He was really the world's best salesman and storyteller. He would weave a story and pull you along for a magic carpet ride, and when you reached the end of the story, his products would conveniently be waiting for you.

He also loved higher education, even though he hadn't earned a degree. I was recruiting content from higher education, but we knew that the iPod was going to live or die with music, and music becomes very important during those college years when you usually form musical tastes that last your whole life. (Red Bull also knew the value of higher ed, and they masterfully built a giant U.S. market by using students as their doorway.) We knew we had a fit with this unique device and music, but we thought if we could get academic content on top of it, like audio textbooks, we could make it ubiquitous. But there was resistance to that, even from within Apple.

There's something called *recency bias*, which says in part that people tend to conclude that the way things are today is the way they will always be. It's hard to see beyond what's in front of your eyes and say, "One day, this will all be different." We love to think we have a bead on what's going on, and oh my do we love to be right! But that's dangerous for someone in sales, because your job is to sell the future—the invisible, the not-yet-built. You have to think ahead.

Steve's greatest gift was his ability to not only think that way but to sell his vision, and he had to do it internally just as much as he did to the outside world. Great leaders spend as much time selling in-house as they do externally. Often, poor leaders and bad managers just dictate internally because they can: "Do it this way or you're fired." They end up with automatons who don't bring any creativity or enthusiasm to the work because they don't understand why they're doing it.

Steve would sell those of us inside Apple with the same energy that I might use to sell someone at a university on why they should switch from Windows to Mac. But he knew something most leaders don't even consider. As a sales pro, you know part of selling is dealing with objections. People resist change, and part of your job is to weave a story that makes change exciting and pregnant with possibility, not scary or expensive. But in outside sales, objections are usually vocal and obvious: "You're not standard; IT doesn't understand you; we don't care about unboxing experiences." And so on. You hear them, and you can counter them.

But when they're dealing with their internal team, many company leaders and VPs of sales conveniently overlook the fact that while people might have objections and really good questions, they don't voice them out of fear of being shouted down or even punished. So the CEO or VP takes silence as a sign of acquiescence and doesn't even bother to sell the employees. "Just do it" might be a great slogan if you're selling shoes, but it's a pretty worthless mission statement if you're staking your reputation on a project you think is a dead end.

Steve never assumed that people got it. He wove compelling stories about human creativity and the potential of technology like a scout leader sitting around a campfire, and by the time he was done, you were on board. You believed. You were ready to take on the world and show them what they were missing.

Sony Corporation didn't have a Steve, and there's no way to know what that's cost them. But the truth is that Sony had every piece of the iPod in house before Apple introduced it. It's true. They had the hardware, the software, and the music rights. They owned BMI, the music publishing and licensing entity, for heaven's sake! They could have (and probably *should* have) beaten Apple to market with the iPod by a couple of years. And still, they missed out. Apple created the iPod. Sony didn't. Why?

I found out why when I met Sony's product manager for digital devices at the American Council on Education (ACE) conference in Washington D.C. That's the president's council, where all the university college presidents go. When she learned who I was, she was a little standoffish, but we sat down and chatted. The iPod had been out for about two months and was the talk of the town.

Finally I said, "How did this happen?"

She knew what I meant. "Well, we were struggling with getting BMI to license the content," she said.

This was dumbfounding. I said, "But you own BMI."

She shrugged. "They have their business models, and we have our business models." And that was it. In one sentence, she summed up the barrier that prevented Sony from leading what became a $6 billion market in the U.S. alone by 2007—the year the first iPhone came out.

But that wasn't the real problem. Sony had no Steve. There was no one there to crystallize a vision for them. Nobody to sell them internally on a new journey. Everybody was doing their own thing. Steve got us all on the same journey, with zero departure from message. When he came back, presentation templates were distributed. If you changed the template, other than putting in the factual material for your audience, it was a fireable offense.

Steve did all that with storytelling. Storytelling is the heart of music, and it was at the core of what we did in selling Apple.

A Few Words on...Character

If you listen to the greatest storytelling songs in pop, rock, folk, or blues, there's always a character at the center. Robert Johnson going to the crossroads to sell his soul. Sgt. Pepper and his Lonely Hearts Club Band. Billie Joe MacAllister, who jumped off the Tallahatchie Bridge. That's important, because we relate to other people. We see ourselves in them. When you're sharing a story with a customer, put character at the center, even if it's not them. To matter, any story needs something to be at stake—something that could be gained or lost depending on the decisions the character makes. If you want people engrossed in your story, make it about someone, and have stakes that the listener can appreciate.

Emotion and Tension

Music is storytelling. Go back to first century England, Ireland, Scotland, and Wales and you'll find *bards*, storytellers and musicians who spread the oral traditions of a tribe or village. Later, after stories started to be written down, bards became wandering minstrels, traveling through the countryside bearing the news of the day but also the stories and legends that filled the long nights. They were historians, and the words told the story, but the music set the mood and the emotion.

That tradition led to the creation of ballads—folk songs that related narratives, usually about larger-than-life characters like Robin Hood, Paul Bunyan, and John Henry. But storytelling through music also has a tradition in the classical world—not only in opera, where words are sung in the form of a libretto, but also in instrumental classical music. If you know anything about the works of masters like Bach or Mozart, you know classical pieces include "phrases," "motifs," and "themes," just as you might find in written stories.

From fairy tales to epics like *The Odyssey*, storytelling is as old as humanity, and it has its tropes and go-to conventions that are still with us. There are broad sensual metaphors (what linguists and historians call *formulas*): the hero's journey, the "rule of three" (three riddles, three brothers, three wishes, that sort of thing) and other standard equipment that no storyteller should be without. But at its heart, all storytelling has two fundamental objectives:

1. Communicate emotion.
2. Convey the rise and release of tension.

Will Romeo kill himself before he figures out that nitwit Juliet isn't really dead? Will Luke Skywalker blow up the Death Star before Vader takes him out? Everything is about our emotions in the presence of rising tension and the resolution of that tension. Great storytellers make it clear what's at stake, stoke that tension until it's nearly unbearable, and then offer a release of tension. That's what makes great stories so cathartic.

For example, 1970's "Layla" by Derek and the Dominos is a great song all by itself, but it becomes a hundred times more poignant when you know the backstory: Eric Clapton, who wrote and sang the tune, was madly in love with Patti Boyd, who was married to George Harrison. Yeah, *that* George Harrison. You can hear the pain and longing of unrequited love in the famous piano part that forms the second half of the song.

Steve was a master at evoking emotion and stoking tension, and his brilliance at this set the tone for Apple. Everything he did was the polar opposite of the so-called leadership that nearly destroyed the company. For instance, after I first joined Apple, CEO John Sculley came to Tallahassee to speak to the Florida Economic Conference. I drove him to the event, and he said maybe ten words to me. He got out, did his little canned speech, put a videotape on, and everyone watched footage about something called the "Knowledge Navigator." Nobody knew what the hell "Knowledge Navigator" was, much less what we were supposed to do with it. Then Sculley got back in his car, was driven to the airport, and left. That was the pattern. Every time we had a national or global sales conference, the CEO *du jour* would walk out, read off prepared slides, and leave.

Wow. The inspiration. Be still my heart.

When Steve came back, he attended the next global sales conference in Santa Clara, California, and I'll never forget it. The contrast couldn't have been more obvious. He walked out on stage where there was one stool, three bottles of water, a mic stand, and a mic. He pulled the stool over, sat down, and said, "Any questions?"

No slides, no presentation, nothing. It was simple but electric, because he wasn't putting in an obligatory appearance. He was there to engage with us, like a storyteller ready to weave a tale. He didn't have somewhere more important to be. That day, we had a dialogue, and he did something that no CEO had done in the nine years that I'd been with Apple: he *listened*. Then he moved to, "Here's what we're going to do." And he took us on a journey.

The Sonic Backdrop to the Customer Story

The greatest thing Apple has always had going for it is the Cult of Mac. That's why iTunes was released to Mac only first. We knew when we stepped into the Windows world, things were going to get complex and bitchy. And anal. And polyester. And we were used to cotton. Silk, even. But the big reason was the cult of personality.

People talk about the cult of personality with Steve. But it was actually a cult of *customer* personality. To this day, the hardcore Apple customers are still a tribe. They're different and they know it. They feel a kinship with Apple, and even back then, before the iPhone made Apple the most coveted brand on Earth, Steve understood the value of their feedback like no chief executive I've ever seen, before or since.

Apple's fans weren't just customers. They were our partners. They were characters in our story, and they even had a hand in writing that story. That meant everything. They weren't just buying products; they were coming along for the ride. They weren't sitting in focus groups, because Steve despised focus groups, but we knew what was on their minds. They weren't just using a product; this was part of their life, and I saw that every day. Being part of the cult was part of their identity and their own story—how they defined and differentiated themselves from those soulless IBM and Windows users.

Steve absolutely understood the power of telling a company story and giving the customer the freedom to define their role in that story. If you want to make selling effortless, that's critical. If you can invite the customer to join you on your journey, to help them feel that they are not only with you but actually shaping the journey in real time, you have their loyalty. You become more than a seller of solutions. You elevate your audience.

I've seen it in music. Audiences clapping and cheering in unison, singing along, transported by the words and the melody. I've seen it at Coachella, at SXSW, at clubs, and at stadium shows. They stop being ticket buyers and become part of the show.

That was one of the big reasons we rolled out the iPod on campuses before we debuted it anywhere else. Steve and the thirty-five of us in Higher Education sales knew that in youth culture—and especially on a college campus—there's always a driving need to have your music.

When you're young (and even when you're not) music is a part of your story. People tend to file the distinct periods of their lives based on three factors: who they were in a relationship with, what kind of job they had, or what kind of music they were into. How many times have you looked back on a time in your life and thought, "That was the summer I was listening to so-and-so"? It doesn't matter if it's Van Morrison or Kendrick Lamar. What matters is that the music touched you and stayed in your memory when other things and people fell away. It's the soundtrack to your life story. How can music *not* affect us?

When I joined Apple, we were still in the age of the mix tape. People wanted their music, and they wanted it portable—at the time, on cassette tapes. More on that later, but the irony was that Sony owned the portable cassette player market, first with the Walkman and then the Discman. What Apple did with the iPod was to make music even more personal. The iPod was about *your* music. You could program it to be the backdrop to whatever your story was that day or that month.

Our customers were already musicians, and the funny thing is that in the early discussions about the iPod, it wasn't going to be a consumer device or a separate product. It was going to be an appendage for the Mac. Fortunately, we came to our senses when we saw the power that music had to enhance the story our customers were already telling about themselves. Even if you didn't play an instrument, the iPod made you a musician.

That's why iTunes was a success—six hundred thousand people immediately bought into the idea and immediately sent us feedback. That was the size of the initial demo. By day four, we had six hundred thousand cult members telling us what we did right and wrong. That was a little overwhelming, but it was absolute validation that we were doing it right. Because there was no connection like that between Microsoft and Windows users, and there still isn't. Today, Android users don't feel a bond with Google or Samsung. They're not part of a bigger narrative. But they are with Apple.

What's Your Story?

In a 2007 article in *Harvard Business Review*, Peter Guber, chairman and CEO of Mandalay Entertainment, said, "...the ability to articulate your story or that of your company is crucial to almost every phase of enterprise management. It works all along the business food chain. A great salesperson knows how to tell a story in which the product is the hero. A successful line manager can rally the team to extraordinary efforts through a story that shows how short-term sacrifice leads to long-term success. An effective CEO uses an emotional narrative about the company's mission to attract investors and partners, to set lofty goals, and to inspire employees. Sometimes a well-crafted story can even transform a seemingly hopeless situation into an unexpected triumph."[1]

That's one hundred percent true. If you're not telling the story of your company or your products through your sales and marketing, you're leaving money and market share on the table. For us in sales, the Apple story was like the vanguard of an army, clearing the way for us when we sat down for a meeting. People were half sold before we even arrived—not every time, but more often than not.

If you're an individual account executive calling on customers, you need to tell the story of your product, your company, and how your product will make the customer's life better. If you're leading a sales department or running a business, you need a story that tells customers who you are and what your company stands for. In other words, writing and sharing your story are essential components of selling.

What is your story? That depends. It could be the story of how your company started and the people who founded it—the story of Woz and Jobs in the garage building the Apple I (well, it was Woz who built it, but that's a tale for another time). It could be the story of overcoming crises, recessions, or other obstacles to make the company what it is. It could be the story of how your prod-

---

1   Peter Guber, "The Four Truths of the Storyteller, *Harvard Business Review,*
     December 2007, https://hbr.org/2007/12/the-four-truths-of-the-storyteller.

uct came to be, has evolved, and what it can do for the customer. Over more than two decades of sitting down with university presidents, chancellors, provosts, and IT people, I had many stories I could tell. I'd talk about Apple's long history of collaborating with higher education. I'd walk the listener through how Apple's technology could transform their student experience and campus culture. I might paint a picture of how the products they were considering would evolve and how their input could be part of that evolution.

By weaving a story, I moved past the perception of a sales call as coercive and predatory (the lowest form of selling) and created an experience that was transparent and aspirational for the customer. I revealed who Apple was and who I was. I showed them that I understood their goals, both organizational and personal. If you want to stop worrying about objections forever, do one thing: tell an honest story about your product and company that makes your customer the hero.

This is what storytelling can do for you in a selling situation:

- **Reveal who you and your company are.** People don't buy from companies but from other people. When there's trust between seller and customer, that greases the wheels of any transaction. One of the best ways to build that trust is to be open about your values and the values and character of the company you work for. Tell a story that reveals those values and character in clear terms, and make sure it's verifiable (because your prospect *will* check on it). People want to feel like they know a company and understand its soul, and that's easier when, instead of hearing you say, "Oh yeah, we care about the community," they hear about the time your managers and employees teamed up to send a local Little League team to Washington, D.C.

- **Reveal the price you've paid to get here.** File this one under "the better they know you, the more likely they'll buy from you" too. Everyone has sacrificed to get where they are, but when your story makes it clear the price that you, your bosses, or your company as a whole have paid to grow, be ethical, or survive tough times, you reveal even more about your collective and individual character. Don't be maudlin in your storytelling, and for heaven's sake, don't fabricate something, but if there's a story of overcoming great odds or giving up dreams to fulfill duty, lean into it.

• **Create cool, especially if your company is boring**. We had an advantage at Apple: we were cool. I don't mean I was cool—unless you count the monkey-mayonnaise thing, I'm pretty boring. But Apple, even in our misbegotten beige box days, had an aura that made selling easier because people want to associate with what's cool. But what if your company sells bolts, animal parts for making dog food, or tires? Find the story and you can make cool out of nothing. Talk about some of the buildings your fasteners hold together. Talk about how the founders of your company raised champion hunting hounds. Talk about the science of how your tires hold Formula One cars to the racetrack. Suddenly, your customer's not scrolling through her phone while you're talking. She's on the edge of her seat, paying attention.

• **Show the customer your "why."** In his classic book, *Start with Why*, Simon Sinek writes, "Very few people or companies can clearly articulate WHY they do WHAT they do. ... By WHY I mean your purpose, cause or belief—WHY does your company exist? WHY do you get out of bed every morning? And WHY should anyone care? ... People don't buy WHAT you do, they buy WHY you do it."[2] *Precisely*. Stories tell your customer why your company does what it does—why you, the human being sitting across from them, do what you do. When we understand why someone made the choices they

---

2   Simon Sinek, *Start with Why: How Great Leaders Inspire Everyone to Take Action,* (New York: Portfolio Books, 2011), (39, 41).

made and why they're where they are, we know them. We're connected. That's how the best sales happen.

- **Let people know what's at stake**. The customer doesn't care about your commission; they care about whether or not what you're selling will deliver value that justifies the cost. One way to get across that divide is to let the customer know what's at stake if they don't buy from you. You do that with storytelling. With Apple, it was easy for us to shape a narrative of what might happen if a university stayed with the IBM/Windows platform: stagnation, obsolescence, other colleges leapfrogging them by giving their students new Apple laptops, etc. Storytelling lets you communicate the risks of not buying from you in a way that doesn't feel threatening. You're just talking about a possible future.

The Parts of a Story

I wanted to be a part of a good story as much as my customers did. I wanted to be with the plasma physicist who was doing something unique with Apple servers that nobody had ever thought about doing. I wanted to be with those kinds of people because they were doing new and exciting things. But telling a great story means understanding what makes a story. It begins with the *setup*.

Before you can take anyone—a customer, a subordinate, a friend—on a journey, you have to lay out the world they're journeying through. Think about the first fifteen minutes of a film. The director's job is to let you know who the main characters are, what their motivations are, where and when the story takes place, and what the rules are. In the classic song "Me and Bobby McGee" (the best-known version was recorded by Janis Joplin), songwriter Kris Kristofferson does this immediately. He lets us know that the characters are stuck in Baton Rouge, Louisiana, they're broke, they're waiting for a train, and that one of them is named Bobby McGee. It's hard to imagine a quicker or more vivid setup.

In the story of your company or product, who are the players? What's the time and place? What's the backdrop of culture or circumstances the story plays out against? Is there a ticking clock? The better your setup, the better your story will land.

Next comes the *conflict*. Every good story hinges on two things: what the main character wants and the obstacles that stand in the way of him getting it. The conflict between the character and those obstacles *is* the story. Frodo wants to destroy the One Ring, but the armies of the Dark Lord are in his way. In *The Godfather*, Michael Corleone wants to escape his crime family, but the pressure to take over the empire finally becomes too great. In Joni Mitchell's song "Free Man in Paris," the protagonist (record executive and future DreamWorks co-founder David Geffen) talks about how he wishes he could stay a carefree Parisian traveler, but he's pulled back by the demands of the recording industry.

To locate the conflict in your story, first decide which story you're leading with. Your company's? The product's? Your own? Then look for the bumps in the road, the catastrophes or reversals that you or your company had to get past to get where you are today. For a company, that might mean anything from fighting co-founders to funding troubles to your CEO being ousted and replaced by a bunch of empty suits. If you're talking about your own conflict, make sure it's relevant to why you're sitting in front of your customer at that moment—say, the many strange and difficult career paths you went down before getting into sales.

Conflict creates drama and tension. Don't leave the office without it.

Next, we have the *story arc*. If you know anything about theater or film, you know that every script is supposed to have a three-act story arc. The first act is the setup, followed by a turning point that sends us into the second act. The second act sees the conflict play out in various ways, ending in a turning point that brings us to the climax of the conflict in the third act. The third act puts the main character in a final, decisive confrontation with the obstacle and brings the conflict to its resolution. Blackout.

Your story needs a beginning, middle, and end. With a strong setup, the beginning is covered. But you'll need to transition the middle part—where the characters interact and interesting stuff happens—or your listener's eyes will glaze over. Then you'll need to move to some sort of payoff where you make the big sale, the company is saved, or some other dramatic climax. That payoff is what allows the listener to release tension and feel satisfaction; it's part of the natural rhythm of storytelling.

Finally, we have the *lesson*. Now, not all stories in all environments have lessons attached to them. In fact, most good stories don't, because lessons quickly become preachy and artificial. But you're selling, and you want your customer to take away something more than, "What a great story!" from your meeting. The object of weaving a story is to help the customer understand you and your company—and eventually, to make the sale.

To do that, you need to prime your audience on what to think and how to feel about the story you've just told. This takes finesse; you can't just say, "Bob, that story illustrates why Consolidated has the strongest family values in our industry." Thud. That's a dropped stick or a broken guitar string. Good lessons are subtle but clear—statements like, "Coming back from the brink of bankruptcy taught our founders that you can't take tomorrow for granted—that you have to keep reinventing yourself." And that's it. Drop your lesson and let the customer pick it up.

Oh, and there's one more piece of a good story that I have to mention before we move on. *Brevity*. A good story is a short story. Make it strong but keep it tight. Better to leave your customer wanting more than to be the one who hangs around too long at the party until your hosts are silently wishing you'd go home.

What the Marvel Cinematic Universe and the Apple Store Have in Common

Not knowing how to tell your story can handicap you in ways that aren't always clear. The biggest mistake I see is that company leaders and account executives forget that people are always the heartbeat of any story. Without people, the audience doesn't care.

Bear with me through this analogy. Unless you've been living in a remote monastery, you know that, for better or worse, we're living through the Age of the Superhero Movie. I'm not a big fan of the genre, but it's instructive because there are two competing visions of what one of those movies should look like: Marvel versus DC. Their contrasting choices for how to tell a story say a lot about their success.

You can't argue that the Marvel Cinematic Universe (MCU) is the more successful of the two, punctuated by the mammoth success of this year's *Avengers: Endgame*. MCU films are almost always centered on the characters, and the action springs from the character's emotions, motivations, history, and choices. Audiences respond to them because, while Iron Man and Captain America have extraordinary abilities, at their core, they're people.

DC's films have mostly been different: focused on action set pieces and digital effects. It seems like the people in the stories are either stereotypes or forgettable. The two exceptions to this pattern, *Wonder Woman* and *Shazam!*, are, not coincidentally, DC's most successful movies. Effective storytelling is always, always about people. If it's not, something has to change.

One of the things that frustrated me about Adobe and the startups that I worked with was that they didn't know who they were. They didn't know how to tell their story. They hadn't given any thought to it or didn't think it mattered. They thought that their products would make their value so self-evident that customers would flock to buy. But that's wrong. Worse, it's leaving a major sales arrow in your quiver, unused.

One of the things that was brilliant about Steve Jobs was that he was able to put himself in the minds of the people who were part of the Apple tribe. He could insert himself into the story, whether it was higher education, the dealer channel, the people who were selling our products, or the consumer world at the retail level. When he put himself into the minds of consumers, that's what birthed the Apple Store.

Not long after he took over again in 1997, we had an education sales meeting where he said of our dealer channel, "They're not telling our story properly." And when he announced that Apple would open its own retail stores, you could hear the entire audience gasp. That was, of course, attacking our consumer sales channel, and that's something no sane company does. You don't undermine the retailers who are selling your products by going into competition with them.

Unless, of course, you're Apple. Steve didn't like how retailers like Best Buy, Circuit City, CompUSA, and Office Max were representing our products. We had these "store within a store" concepts that were weak half measures. Steve was right: Apple was about a journey, the identity of the user, and music. There wasn't any music in third-party retailers, and they didn't know or care about telling our story. We would build our own music studio.

Oh yeah, we were nervous. Remember that there were no iPods or iPhones yet, and most of the business we were doing was in education—$3.2 billion worth. The consumer side of the business was a relative blip. Many education accounts and students bought from authorized dealers—independent stores that could sell at a reduced price to students, faculty, and staff. So someone asked, "Well, how's that going to, you know, affect our one-on-one relationship with the dealers?" Steve said, "It'll probably put them out of business." Another gasp and a lot of nervous subsonic chatter. That was Steve in a nutshell: fearless, disruptive, and totally merciless with things that weren't working.

Steve wanted environments that would represent the Apple story, and that wasn't a story where selling was everything. Nobody at an Apple Store ever walks up and says, "Can I help you find something?" because everyone knows that's code for, "What do you want to buy, and can I ring you up so I get the commission?" People hate sales pressure, and there isn't any at Apple Stores. You can hang out there all day and play and nobody will bother you. Even Starbucks will ask you to buy a grande Americano after a while.

The first store opened in Palo Alto, California, near Stanford, in 2001, and educators and students were the first customers. Ron Johnson came over from Target to run the stores, and then left us and went over to J.C. Penney, where...things didn't work out so well. But Ron brought the Apple Store to fruition brilliantly; he was the real genius behind them. Maybe my next book will be about what he did. Because Steve, Tim Cook, and Ron were the triumvirate who fixed Apple.

Naturally, our legacy dealers were furious about all this, but if you think about it, the move makes perfect sense. Apple and a vanilla reseller like Circuit City were never going to be a fit; that's why the "store within a store" thing flopped. But Apple Stores became a physical manifestation of Apple's story, especially when you fast forward to the crazy days after the introduction of the iPhone when people would line up and camp out for days to be among the first to get the new model. The stores became Ground Zero for that excitement, and that's what Steve had in mind.

If you want to understand the world I lived in for twenty-two years, it was that high-touch world. The world where you never argued over price, and the conversation was always about value. When people said they couldn't afford Apple, they just didn't understand the value proposition. When you look at Apple Stores today, that hasn't changed. Steve always thought computing was too hard, and the Apple Stores are a place where it's made easier. That's why we created the Genius Bars.

The stores are a place to take care of the faithful, but also to indoctrinate new members of the tribe. Each store is a church, and gorgeous design, ease of use, and effortless functionality are the gospel. Like a church, the intention is to tell a story that hits you where you live, take you on a journey, and then save you. The difference is that Apple will save you with a CPU, an LCD, and some spectacular software. Amen.

An Annoying Musical Interlude

Sometimes, the song isn't so much the story as how the song came to be. The immortal Pink Floyd song Shine On You Crazy Diamond is actually about original lead singer Syd Barrett who, in 1967 and 1968, started acting very strangely—either from years of dropping LSD (including mixing the drug into hair gel and then standing under the stage lights so the heat would make his scalp—and somehow his brain—absorb the acid faster), schizophrenia, or both. He left the band and was replaced by David Gilmour, but legend has it that when Pink Floyd was at London's famous Abbey Road studios recording the tune in 1975, Syd showed up and was unrecognizable. One famous account of that day has Syd trying to brush his teeth by jumping up and down while holding his arm still. In a tribute to their far-gone former bandmate, Roger Waters and the rest of Pink Floyd dedicated Crazy Diamond to Syd.

The lesson: Everybody is living a story. You probably know nothing about it, and it might be a more difficult, painful, or challenging story than you could imagine. Remember that and respect the story you haven't yet heard.

Everything and Everyone Is the Story

The church analogy makes me laugh, because Steve was like an evangelical cult leader, and if you think the cult only existed among Apple customers, you don't know the half of it. Apple was a cult internally, too. You could say that we drank the coffee instead of the Kool-Aid, because the first thing Steve did when he came back was make the coffee free in Café Mac. He said, "People are going to be working very late hours, and I want to make sure they have all the coffee they can consume."

Of course, no one knew what was in the coffee. Hmm...

I haven't been to the new headquarters in Cupertino that everyone calls The Spaceship (and it's possible that after this book I never will), but when I was a field salesperson, going to the old HQ was almost a religious pilgrimage. The fascinating thing about Apple corporate was that the magic was just as palpable at the office as it was at the Apple Stores. I'm not Catholic, but I went to Catholic schools, and when you go through a Catholic mass and see the pomp and ritual, and then you go behind the altar and see the Host and the communion wine stuffed in a cardboard box—the mystique is gone.

That never happened at Apple HQ, in part because the story was always consistent, but also because we were all part of writing it. Everyone at Apple, from accounting to customer service to order entry, knew the story and felt like it reflected us too. It wasn't something handed down from management. Remember, the very first thing Steve did when he came back and had a meeting with us was *listen*. (More on that in the next chapter.) He didn't throw out a few bullshit questions and then wait for safe answers. The man sat down on a stool and said, "Any questions?" He respected us. He wanted to hear what we had to say and to contribute our part to the song, not just play his own tune.

That changed everything about Apple—changed our music. There was a different feel in the hallways, a different energy in meetings. We were alive again. From sales to software to product development to marketing, we'd always known that Apple needed to take back its disruptive mojo if we were ever going to be great again, but management wouldn't listen. They dictated their story. Steve was a leader, and while he very much had his own story in mind, it was a story that we all felt like we were a part of and could influence.

I liken it to when I left my narrow disco world, driving north on US 19 to Tallahassee, Florida. On a college radio station, WANM-FM, late at night, I heard my first real blues song. And I said, "What is this? This is an amazing rhythm track. This has heart, it's different than what I've been playing." With the music I'd been playing in discos, I could have left the stage in the middle of a song to go to the bathroom and nobody would've known I was gone.

Suddenly, with the blues, there was heart, soul, pain, and re-demption. That's what it was like with Steve. It stopped being about the products or the faceless rotation of CEOs and became about all of us again. Yes, our success was also due to brilliant marketing and fantastic technology, especially after the iOS era began. But it was really because we rediscovered our music and our story. That's why Apple doesn't feel like any other company. When you walk into an Apple Store and an employee in jeans and a T-shirt says, "How's it going?" it feels different. It's hard to express, but we had it, and Steve let us go back to it.

A Few Words on...Humor

Do you think I'm funny? If you said no, then you're wrong, because I'm hysterical. Just ask me. By the way, I'll be here until Thursday. Be sure to try the veal, and tip your waitstaff! Okay, that was a long way to go to make a point, but the point is, humor is very much in the eye of the beholder. Humor is also a very important part of storytelling and songwriting, though in my opinion too many songwriters take their craft way too seriously. (Check out the music of Barenaked Ladies for one example of songwriters who appreciate levity in a lyric.) Humor is like salt: powerful but only good when applied with restraint. Steve was too intense and driven to be a jokester; he was more like James Brown, who would fine his bandmates for screwing up a note or dance step in rehearsal. You don't drop a joke on someone like that.

The lesson: Get to know the person across the table or the audience in front of the stage before you crack wise. Humor can open doors or slam them.

What You'll Need to Create Your Epic Ballad

Framing—Framing might be the most important function of story. Your story lends context and perspective to events so you can see the larger narrative arc running through them. When you apply a frame to disconnected events, you connect them as part of a larger tale. Let's say the first year of your startup was a comedy of missteps and disasters, something that's pretty common. If you don't put that year into the frame of a larger story, it remains nothing more than a series of screwups. But when you frame it as a story, with a common thread running through it like perseverance or optimism, you turn those errors into part of a dramatic hero's journey.

A framed narrative says something about you, your company, or your products. It tells people who you are, what you care about, what you'll do to succeed, what you won't stand for...a lot of things. That's not just for external consumption either. If you're a manager or executive, your people need to know your company story. That's what lends meaning to the long hours and the sacrifice. If your people feel like they're part of a great narrative that's still playing out—a narrative that can have an impact on the world—they'll walk through fire for you.

Perspective—An important part of psychological maturity is *theory of mind*—the realization that everyone around you has their own complex inner life that's as real and vital to them as yours is to you. In other words, everybody's the star of their own story. In order to craft a story that impacts people and that they will adopt as their own, you need to respect that reality.

Steve did that with Apple. There were no small players in our story. Everyone played a role in creating the culture. When you're developing your own sales story, respect the fact that the person sitting across from you has their own story, and you're just a bit player in it, just as they're a bit player in yours. That's so crucial I'll repeat it.

When you call on a customer, they are a stepping stone for you in your story, something that you're using to reach a goal. Sure, they might also be someone you know and like, but they have a purpose in your narrative. *You're the same thing for them.* In their minds, your roles are reversed. They have goals and dreams, and what you're selling is just one component in getting to those goals and dreams. Remember that and account for it, and you'll shape your narrative in a way that puts your customer front and center. Respecting their inner life is the key to their heart...and their signature.

Reasons—I was going to call this one "Relevance," until I realized that was missing the point. When you make something relevant, you're simply drawing a line that connects your story to the listener. That's important, but it also disrespects their intelligence by telling them what your story is supposed to mean. That's for them to decide. Just as you don't get to claim that you're a great drummer or singer or bass player—the audience decides that—the people listening to your story determine what it means *for them*.

No, I chose *reasons* because they're about your "why," as we talked about before. What's the reason this story is useful for your audience? Why do they need to hear it? What can they never hope to grasp about your company, your products, or you without listening to it?

That said, you also need to make your story relevant to the people who consume it. That doesn't mean changing the details for each audience; that's pandering. Instead, know the values of all your stakeholders and craft a story that relates to those values. Apple's story was music and unrestrained, joyful creativity. If you're selling cars, your story might be about your love of classic cars or road trip stories. If you're selling real estate, your story might turn on growing up in the area and watching how it's changed over the years.

But don't forget a reason. If your reason for being in real estate is that you want to help shape how the community grows because of what it means to you, that's gold.

The Road to the Stage—Manager

You should have your rehearsal space and routine in place, and if you do, it's time to start crafting stories. Not every band writes its own music, but cover bands are like unimaginative companies: one in a multitude, quickly forgotten. Be an original, and write your story. Even if you're not ready to compose actual songs, have a clear idea of the characters and motivations that you want to write about. Know the ups and downs that make the story interesting. Remember, your story is fascinating to you because it's about you, and you were there for it. To someone else, it's secondary to their story. Great songwriters and storytellers find universal themes in their stories—love, heartbreak, struggle, hard choices—that they know their listeners can relate to. Find the universal themes in the story of your company or products. Then craft a series of stories for every occasion—a sales meeting, a conference speech, a sit-down over drinks with a potential hire.

The Road to the Stage—Individual Contributor

You're a member of the band, and you might not feel like a songwriter or storyteller. But trust me, when you're part of a group and you're creating original music, everybody plays a role. The drummer may not write the words or melody, but nobody is better qualified to lay down the tempo of a new song or determine what the feel will be. Short and sharp? A relaxed, loping Texas shuffle? A thundering power ballad? You have a role to play in your company's story because you have a unique set of experiences.

What about your own story, independent of your company? That starts when you look back on the events of your life and career and see the patterns: the triumphs, the tragedies, the comebacks, etc. What's the consistent theme? Once you know, that's the heart of your story. Have you always been the overlooked underdog? The misunderstood artist? The loving son of a great dad? That's where the narrative begins.

Rock, Jazz, or Something Else

Music and story go hand in hand. One will reveal a great deal about the other. One of the tests I used to do in hiring salespeople for the startups I worked for was to say, "Show me your playlist." I'd get the strangest looks that said, "Are you for real?"

But the music someone listens to tells me a lot about them and their story. Are they stylistically open? Do they pick decent music? One person I hired when I was at littleBits went from Bruno Mars to B.B. King to Sister Sledge to classical. I mean here is somebody who's eclectic and worldly, open to new ideas. I hired her right away.

Remember, music is the soundtrack to the story of people's lives, and the soundtrack to the companies that people build. Pay attention to the music and you can learn a lot about the story they're telling themselves.

Michael's Excruciating Storytelling To-Do List:

- Learn your history. What are the components of your story or your company's story? The ups, the downs, the wins and losses, the major players? Retrace the steps you took to get where you are—people, opportunities, setbacks, etc. Those are the raw material of the story.

- Ignore the audience...for now. Like I said earlier, if you want to be truly original, you can't create with your audience in mind. You have to write your story to please yourself. The time will come to consider the audience you'll be playing to, but for now create a story that moves you, period.

- Master the components of the story. This is a matter of feel and repetition. You need to become skilled with the setup, the arc, conflict, and the other critical parts of a good story. Work at it. Field test your story on customers and see what happens. That could be awkward, but it's the only way.

- Nail down your applause lines. Any storyteller, from a standup comedian to a politician, has certain lines designed to get a strong reaction. Learn to feel the "beats" of your story—the transitions when the tension rises or falls or when expectations are turned on their head. Those are the moments to emphasize, because they're when your audience will react and be "all in."

- When the time comes to weave your story, know your audience. Now, tailor the story to your audience by knowing who they are and what they care about. Don't alter the facts to suit the audience; that's cynical and manipulative. However, you can emphasize certain points and dial down others to fit the person and the circumstances.

- Decouple your goals from the story's outcome. Remember, sales isn't selling. It's connecting. Your story should be its own reason for existing, and you should tell it so the listener will understand you or your business and feel there's common ground between you. Full stop. Do not manipulate a story into a sales pitch; that's transparent and a little bit insulting. If your story is true and compelling and you tell it well, you won't need to sell.

CHAPTER 3

Listening

verb

| 'li-sᵊn-ing |

paying attention to sound; hearing something with thoughtful attention

Examples:

Choral singers, orchestral players, vocal jazz combos, improvisers

You might not remember this, which is kind of the point. Steve died in 2011, but Tim Cook's first announcement of a new product didn't happen until the fall of 2015. When the moment came, the product was—ta-da!...

The Apple Pencil. Stop. No, really. Hold your applause.

You can still buy an Apple Pencil, but few people are. The pencil category just wasn't begging to be disrupted. It's not a Newton-caliber flop, but it's not a hit. I would call the Apple Pencil an example of failing to listen to the market. Now, I've said that Steve didn't give a damn what the market said when it came to determining what we would do next or how we would do it, and that's true. But he was great at seeing past hype and accepted wisdom and listening to the subtext of what people wanted. That came through loud and clear at Macworld in 2007 when he announced the debut of the iPhone.

At the time, the Palm Pilot was all the rage among handheld devices (take a beat to think about how much times have changed in just twelve years), and it had a stylus. Naturally, everyone was wondering if the iPhone would come with an iStylus or something. But Steve was having none of it. He loathed the idea of styluses and pencils. "God gave us ten styluses," he roared from the stage. "Let's not invent another one!"

Steve knew that fingers are more dexterous than a stylus, don't get lost, and we don't have to pay for them. They're the natural tools for mobile devices. And he was right. He listened not to what people said but what they wanted. Like any great conductor, Steve was also a great listener who could pick individual notes—right and wrong—out of a cacophony.

Drummers have to be spectacular listeners, especially in a live performance. We're always watching out for someone who's behind the beat or who missed a bar and is moving to the chorus early. My training as a drummer taught me to listen like Steve, and that helped me survive for twenty-two years in a place where many of the senior vice presidents I worked with only lasted six, five, or even three years. I attribute my longevity to being able to "pick up on what people were laying down," to use the vernacular—to hear both their words and the meaning behind them.

That helped me live through six presidents, four CEOs, five vice presidents, and countless sales managers. I'll never forget when my last manager came in and introduced himself. I looked at him and said, "You're number ten." He never got it…but he was gone before I was, so it didn't matter.

To have a great company, you need people with musical minds. In music, at least in a situation where an ensemble is creating the music, everyone adds a piece. It's pure, unstructured collaboration. If you're talking about classical music, the composer is the boss, but in the process of turning those notes on the page into a living, breathing piece of art, many of the musicians in that ensemble will contribute. The oboe player might spot a chord that doesn't work. The timpani player could suggest that, in a certain passage, the tempo or dynamics should change. Everyone has a role. Everyone writes the music.

There's a wonderful passage in the movie *Dead Poet's Society* that expresses what I mean. The character John Keating, played by the late and much missed Robin Williams, is talking to his class about why poetry and passion matter as much as law, medicine and engineering. This is what he says:

> *"That you are here—that life exists, and identity; that the powerful play goes on and you may contribute a verse. That the powerful play goes on and you may contribute a verse. What will your verse be?"*

When Steve came back, we flattened the organization. There were only four people between me and him. That's it. Steve loved the openness of pure research and the experimental atmosphere of higher education, and he wanted to bring a free flow of ideas and knowledge to Apple. So we went from traditional hierarchy to open lines of communication. Steve turned the company into Open Mic Night.

Ever been to an open mic night, say, at your local pub or coffeehouse? It's fun but also pretty Darwinian. People get up and sing or play, and you know right away who's got game and who doesn't. It was like that with Apple. Everybody had a run at the mic, but that meant you could quickly determine who could sing and who couldn't. Who was worth listening to and who wasn't. Yes, Steve gave everybody the stage and let them belt out their song, but he did it in part to reveal who consistently had the best ideas and who could be safely ignored.

I'm not saying you don't need hierarchy in a company. Of course you do. An orchestra is a flat organization because every player has instant access to the CEO—the conductor. Can you imagine playing the oboe and not being able to see the conductor who's leading you? Of course not. That's ridiculous. But there is still status in an orchestra. There are still rankings based on se-niority and ability. You have the first chair violin, for example. That violinist is the de facto leader of the ensemble when the conductor is off stage. In fine cuisine, you have the sous chef.

But hierarchy doesn't preclude communication. It can't, or your organization loses its vitality. If there's too much complexi-ty and distance between leadership and the rank and file, you're like a group of musicians scattered throughout Yankee Stadium, desperately trying to hear each other and failing. The bottom line:

A great ensemble listens, because you never know who will come up with the idea that changes everything about the music you're playing.

The Difference Between Hearing and Listening

I spent years playing studio sessions for Tampa record labels, and that environment will teach you about the importance of listening in no time. Why? Because someone is paying for that studio time, and the longer you take to "get" a song, riff, or harmony, the more it costs them. I learned quickly that hearing and listening are not the same thing.

A few years ago, I ran the education business for Ayah Bdeir at her engineering and robotics startup, littleBits. She was an amaz-ing leader, and one of the things I learned from watching her was the difference between hearing and listening. Hearing is just the receipt of music or information. It's mechanical. There's no pur-pose or understanding behind it. Under the roster of CEOs we had before Steve's return, we in sales (and, I suspect, everyone in every department) were heard, but we rarely felt listened to.

Listening is hearing with empathy, purpose, and respect. You detect nuance and emotion and meaning. You assemble things in your mind that might not be assembled in the real world. That's how music's created. You can hear different notes, but by listening, you figure out how to put them together into a chord. You apply a rhythm. You create harmony. Suddenly, something's there that wasn't there before. You have a song.

Listening is the first step in any kind of innovation, because it means paying attention and being open to what other people and events are telling you—what the subtext is telling you. You can hear that a song is in 3/4 time or cruising along at 120 beats per minute, but you're just taking in information. What does the song mean? Where does it take you? What's the emotion behind it? What is the songwriter trying to say with metaphor and imagery? Listening reveals layers of meaning and awareness—in a song, in a book, in another person. That's how you understand someone and figure out what they want.

At Apple, I knew somebody was listening to us again *before* the first meeting Steve had with sales after his return. Before that, when the sales team came into the room, the audiovisual (AV) guys would always be playing music by The Beastie Boys or some similar group—music that a bunch of twenty-six-year-olds want-ed to hear. We were mostly guys in our forties and fifties, and we didn't relate to that music. But that didn't matter. Nobody was concerned with what we wanted. No one was listening. They were serving themselves.

When I walked into that first meeting with Steve, my musician's ears knew in half a second what was different. The AV guys were playing stuff from our era: Tom Petty, Bruce Springsteen, David Bowie. The effect on the room was electric. The mood was buoyant and energetic. I doubt anybody else in the room was thinking *The music is different! The company cares!* But that didn't matter. They felt the difference. Later, Steve said, "That's the music I want you to play to the audience." He got it.

A Few Words on...Structure

Next time you connect to iTunes or Spotify, turn on Sirius/XM in the car, or just flip on an old-school terrestrial radio (you crazy Luddite!), do something you might not have done before: really listen. Listen to how a rock, pop, hip-hop, or blues song is put together. Listen to how it begins, usually with some sort of percussion hit, followed by an instrumental lead-in. Then, most of the time, you get the usual construction of verse, chorus, verse, chorus, bridge, verse, chorus, and so on. There are variations, but that's not important. What does matter is how that structure affects your experience of the song. Once you recognize the structure, can you predict how you'll feel about the tune and see what the songwriter was doing?

The lesson: Apply that same listening acuity to sales. A sales meeting and a sales pitch also have a structure, but are you aware of what yours is, or have you been going mostly on feel? Break down how you approach a sales call, and you should see the structure. Once you do, you'll see what feels out of place or what isn't working. In other words, once you really listen to the music, you can, in the words of Lennon and McCartney, take a sad song and make it better.

Music Sets the Atmosphere

In selling, you're venturing into hostile territory (sort of) to try to convince someone to spend lots of money on something they may or may not need, and you're not the only one doing it. You need every asset, every ally, every trick that can tip the scales in your favor. One of those, though it's one you're maybe not using, is controlling the atmosphere in the room.

In my current life as a fundraiser for education, I do a lot of presentations. And to this day, whenever I do a presentation that includes a warmup period, I make it a musical one. Here's my simple formula:

- Ascertain the average age of the audience.
- Program music that takes them back to the Billboard charts from when they were eighteen years old.

When you do that in a university environment that is saturated in music, it works. I'll probably do the same thing for my speaking engagements to support this book: have a huge selection of playlists on my iPhone, watch the crowd (if I'm lucky) as they file in, make a guess at their age, and pick a playlist. Thanks to the magic of Bluetooth, we have instant atmosphere. There's a company in New York that just creates audio ambience for restaurants in Manhattan, tailored to the people who go to each specific restaurant.

That reflects what I've said and what Steve used to say all the time about music, design, words, or anything else: "Who's the audience?" If you want to create an environment where people do what you want them to do, you have to know who they are. You do that by listening.

Here are two other things you can do if you want to appreciate how much music—especially when it's in the background—completely changes your listening experience. If you have the technology to do this, try watching a movie like one of the *Star Wars* films without the music. Keep the special effects and dialogue, but drop out the music. College music appreciation classes do this, and it's *weird*. You don't realize how powerfully the music affects your emotions until it's gone. It's like there's a hole in the movie.

If you can't do that, go to one of those events they have at performing arts centers where the symphony orchestra plays the soundtrack of a movie like one of the *Harry Potter* films. When you see the strings playing a certain passage or the timpani or harp creating a musical effect, it gives you a completely new appreciation for how tactile the music is in the films we cherish. There's a *person* behind each of those instruments—sweat, and work, and artistry. It's really moving.

Apple under Steve set free the power of music within the company and in our products. One of the best illustrations of that is the Apple Homepod—the smart speaker that competes with Amazon's Alexa and Google Assistant. Now, I'll be the first to admit that the Homepod isn't as versatile as the others, but its sound quality is leaps and bounds ahead of them. The Homepod is something you buy if you're already part of the Apple ecosystem, but also if you want to fill your home with music. It's for listeners.

The Road to the Stage—Manager

It's essential for the players in a band to listen to each other. That's how you match tempo, achieve dynamic balance, pick up on changes that can inspire solos, know when to come in or keep playing, and so on. But that doesn't mean band members listen to each other all the time. In the rehearsal room, there can be a lot of leaders and few followers. Or, you may have a band member or two who don't like to speak up and so never get heard. Even the most informal bands have a de facto leader—someone who organizes the activity, makes the schedule, and keeps everybody on task. If you're managing a sales team, that's you.

I've already given you a structure for formal times when everyone on your team can get a word in: *rehearsal*. That means regular meetings. They can be casual offsites or official departmental powwows at the office, but what matters is that everyone gets a chance to be heard, and you get a chance to listen. Also, it's just as important to create a culture of listening among your team. Let everyone know that they can come to you with an idea or a concern, whether it's in person, on the phone, or via text, email, Slack, or whatever. Most importantly, listen and act on the information that you take seriously. That builds trust.

The Road to the Stage—Individual Contributor

It's every musician's job to speak up and lend his or her voice to the band's sound. You don't know what will be missing without your contribution. It could be minor, or it could change everything. To get to the stage and play your best, you have to show up ready to make yourself heard.

I get that not everyone is as willing to speak up as I am. For me, the issue is shutting me up and stopping me from telling the same joke fifty-three times. But even if you don't like rocking the boat or raising issues, that doesn't mean you don't want to be heard. Everyone does. So find a way that suits your personality. Speak to your manager in private. Use email. If you're dealing with a customer, talk in a casual setting that's relaxing.

If you're on the other extreme, with a powerful personality and a tendency to overwhelm everyone else, my advice is the same. Choose more private, quieter ways to be heard. Once everyone has their say, the leader's job is to listen and act based on the best information.

Many Kinds of Music, Many Ways to Listen

However, it's a mistake to assume that listening is just about music. It's not. Listening occurs in any environment where people are sharing information about what they want and need as well as how they feel. That information can come in many forms aside from music: spoken words, body language, emotions, actions, and physical appearance, for starters. Even the room you're in or a person's car can speak volumes. The environment is always telling you something, so you should always be paying attention. That's especially relevant in sales, where even the smallest lever could be the one that helps you move the world and close the deal.

In other words, I have my own variation on the Always Be Closing maxim made infamous by the play and movie *Glengarry Glen Ross*: ABL, Always Be Listening. Having your antennae up at all times, even when you think there's nothing to listen to, could make you a lot of money.

One terrific example of that is the coworking behemoth We-Work. I spent a fair amount of time at WeWork locations while writing this book, and I was extremely impressed. Not so much with the revenue model, because WeWork is just real estate arbitrage: lease buildings and carve out office spaces at one price, then rent them to distance workers, independent contractors, and startups at a higher price. I don't think WeWork has a valuation of around $20 billion—with an IPO to come in 2019 as I write this—because of that.

No, WeWork has become a unicorn because of the value add of its design, feel, and community. The company has created a place where people want to be, where they feel part of, if not a family, a circle of close friends. One of the reasons that's happened is that WeWork corporate and its onsite community managers listen to their tenants, including the little guys manning the "hot desks." The company's locations are always putting on events that connect a site's members with the staff and help keep dialogue going.

Also, in a very Apple-like touch, WeWork is obsessive about the small details of its locations and about maintaining its brand integrity. Not a toilet paper roll gets changed out in a location without a blessing from the member experience gods. Signs, wall art, coffee mugs—everything follows a template because it's a template that members really like. WeWork pays attention to the obvious and the not-so-obvious music, such as tracking when their users access certain spaces with their key cards, so management knows what's popular when.

Remember that I told you we built our own CRM solution at Apple? This is why—to listen to the things our customers weren't telling us directly. Even though data collection and mining is no substitute for making a human connection with your customers and developing trust, it's incredibly valuable to gather enough information about the people you're selling to so you can detect the subtle strains of music running through their lives.

It's like detective work—seeing patterns and drawing conclusions. A customer might have a wall covered in nautical memorabilia and books about sailing in his office, leading you to conclude that a surprise gift of a handmade model sailboat or some scrimshaw art (etched ivory or bone) might make a huge impression and win you a lot of points. Another customer could have a pattern of traveling to Edinburgh every August for the International Festival, suggesting that she's a devotee of opera, theatre, and classical music.

There are clues everywhere to what your customers care about and are interested in. You only have to listen to pick up on them and make them part of your strategy.

Believe What You're Hearing

But listening alone isn't enough. Sorry, but it isn't. Don't give me the stink-eye; this chapter will be worth your time. I'm going to tell you what you have to do to as a sales professional to make listening into a powerful part of your toolkit. Two other things:

1. *Believe what you're hearing.*
2. *Act on what you've learned.*

People, particularly salespeople, love to hear themselves talk. And that's okay, but the problem comes when you're only listening to yourself. That probably means you're paying attention to a self-defined reality and not real reality. That's trouble. Take the events that led up to the financial crash of 2008, so well-documented in the book and subsequent film *The Big Short* by Michael Lewis.

At its center, the story of *The Big Short* is about a failure to listen and believing what you want to be true instead. People like Dr. Michael Burry of Scion Capital and Steve Eisman (called Mark Baum in the movie and played wonderfully by Steve Carell) looked at the data involving the housing market and mortgage bonds and realized that a catastrophe was inevitable. That empowered them to bet against the market and make billions after the collapse. But the same information was available to anyone who chose to look.

Why did Burry and Eisman perceive what was about to happen when so few others did?

Because they chose to believe what they were hearing and to act on it. When you're really listening, sometimes you'll hear what you'd rather not. You won't want it to be true. When I was playing drums, there were many times that my band spent hours in rehearsal grinding out a particular tune, only to have it simply not work. The sound, the groove, the mood—something wasn't right. When that happened, we had to believe what we were hearing and drop the song from our set list. The alternative was to bull ahead and play it anyway and risk stinking up the club.

To weaponize listening, you have to believe what the words, actions, and subtext are telling you, whether you like it or not, and then you have to act on that information. That could mean scuttling a favorite project, tearing up a presentation you've spent weeks working on, or even quitting the job you thought you'd love but realize you can't stand. I sympathize; I've been there. But great sales professionals act on what they know, not what they wish was true.

In fact, it's your job to stand up for what your customer wants in the face of what your company thinks the customer *should* want. I can't tell you how many times I had to go back to my bosses at Apple (pre-Steve) and say, "The customer doesn't want this. This isn't the way they do business. They want a single serial number across the entire campus." To their credit, Apple always listened, even when they didn't want to.

I had the same fight with Adobe, and they fought me tooth and nail. They were hearing people but not listening. From the start, they were in the business of selling you a license for your machine. If you wanted to use Photoshop, Illustrator, InDesign, or one of their other products, you paid for a single-seat license. That was the way it had always been done.

Then I came along, fresh from Apple. I wanted to sell a license for an entire campus—all-you-can-eat access to Adobe products at a single, very high price. Why? Because the people who ran this particular university had told me that they didn't want to be in the one-at-a-time license business. I had assembled with a bunch of other people in the university president's board room along with the Chief Information Officer and a bunch of lawyers, and the president stood up and said, "I want to unleash creativity across the entire campus. I want to give everybody Creative Suite. Because I don't know if there's somebody in janitorial services who might be an amazing creative but has never had the tools." It was a bold vision, and I knew what it meant.

But all Adobe heard was, "They want one license." They were like a kid who doesn't understand that if he has one $100 bill, he has more money than the kid who has twenty one-dollar bills. I spent an entire day riding up and down the elevators on Park Avenue in San Jose, talking to legal, to technology, and to myself, trying to get people to understand the value of the deal I was proposing. It was like pulling teeth. Their main concern: "How do we ensure that they don't go over the number of licenses?"

My God, I'm talking about the biggest single deal in the company's history, and they're worried about the customer letting thirty extra people sneak onto Photoshop! Patiently, I told them that the number I was talking about was so big, it wouldn't matter.

Finally, I got the deal done. Full Sail University in Orlando, Florida, bought a single all-access license from Adobe for $13 million per year. Previously, they had been spending $2 million a year on one-at-a-time licenses. This new deal meant that any student with a computer, a password, and access to the university's wireless network could use Adobe Creative Suite. It was the second largest deal in Adobe's history, and it became their business model.

You're welcome, guys.

That deal was the product of listening, believing, and acting. The Full Sail president was listening to the real world of the campus around him. At that time, in 2011, creative work was happening anywhere, and the tools of choice were Apple's hardware and Creative Suite. He knew if he could bring that energy into his institution, he would not only be able to compete with other schools but also have an edge. He acted on that information. I listened to him, believed the deal was possible, and made it happen.

An Annoying Musical Interlude

This isn't actually annoying. It's awesome. In 1971, three young guys were attending Gallaudet University in Washington, D.C., when they decided they wanted to form a rock band. So what, right? Oh, did I forget to mention that Gallaudet is a school for the deaf? That's right, Bob Hiltermann, Ed Chevy, and Steve Longo couldn't hear the music they wanted to play, but they loved rock and roll all the same. So they formed a band with maybe the cleverest name ever: Beethoven's Nightmare. Because, as I'm sure you know, Beethoven was also deaf for much of his life. The great thing is that, a few hiccups notwithstanding, the band has been together for more than forty years, cranking out raging heavy metal, touring, starring in their own documentary, and proving that music really is a universal language.

The lesson: There isn't one, unless it's that you shouldn't let anything tell you that you can't do what you love. But I'm okay with letting the story of three deaf guys in their own heavy metal band stand on its own.

How to Listen

ASK THE RIGHT QUESTIONS

Most of the sales trainings that I've been forced to take against my will (which is pretty much all of them) teach the same thing: "Ask leading questions, and then listen." But that's pretty glib advice that means nothing. When you call on PhDs like I did for nearly twenty-two years, a leading question could turn into a two-and-a-half-hour dissertation.

There's a big difference between asking questions and asking the *right* questions. "What can I do for you today?" is not the right question. It's generic—a silence filler. Good questions come from preparation and understanding context and history. If you don't have a history with the customer, that's fine, but you can still know the context of why you're sitting down. And even if you know nothing, there are still lines of questioning that work in almost any situation. And most of them begin with "Why?"

"Why" questions are the key to selling. I don't care about what someone wants to buy or how much they want to spend until I know why I'm sitting across from them. What are their goals? What are their challenges? What pain are they trying to relieve? Is this personal and if so, why? The right questions will almost always begin as a quest to find out someone's motivations and beliefs. After that, you can design a solution to satisfy them. If you focus on questions about what, when, and how much, you're just an order taker.

BE QUIET AND LISTEN WITHOUT JUDGMENT

A wise man once said, "People want to tell their story. Shut up and let them tell it." In all my years of selling, I've never seen anything to contradict that statement. People want to be heard, and if you ask the right questions and give them space to get comfortable with opening up to you, they will tell you their story, often in greater detail than you ever thought possible. But only if you shut up and listen without judgment.

What does that mean? Ask, and then stop talking. Get comfortable with the silence that follows, knowing that the other person is preparing internally to respond. Make and maintain eye contact, but keep your expression neutral no matter what the other person says. Most people will only open up if they feel they can speak without being judged. Don't interrupt, and don't react. Just listen. Be an interviewer on *60 Minutes*: impartial, calm, and cool. But while you're being calm and cool, be thinking about your follow-up questions.

True, some people hate to be put on the spot and hate to talk. But eventually, everyone opens up. It might take a long time or even multiple meetings, but keep at it—calm, inviting, non-judgmental. Think like a safecracker. You'll get them.

PAY ATTENTION TO WHAT'S NOT SAID, BECAUSE THE MARKET DOES KNOW WHAT IT *NEEDS*

Steve always used to say that the market didn't know what it wanted, but I think he misspoke. What he was really saying was that the market might not be able to tell you what it wants, but it knows what it needs; and it will tell you in unspoken clues if you know what to look for. Steve read the frustration with other MP3 players like the Zune—with their poor storage, terrible controls, and lame user experience—and knew that while the market wasn't asking for the iPod, it clearly needed it.

It's the same in sales. What's not said is always more powerful and revealing than what is said. Be alert to nuance and subtle cues in the subtext. Has your customer omitted something from a statement that you already know from another source? (This is great justification for doing your research.) Why? Do their emotions match their words when they speak, and if not, why? There's a world of knowledge to be gained from the unsaid, and a great account executive takes advantage.

KEEP YOUR B.S. METER RUNNING

I wish everyone was honest and truthful all the time, but they're not. I know I'm not. Michel Hageloh isn't even my real name...or is it? Seriously, you can't get so caught up in listening and respecting every word everyone says that you take everything at face value. You know this. You have to maintain a balance between empathetic, analytical listening and healthy skepticism.

I follow two pretty basic rules when it comes to what I hear, and they've served me well. First, if it seems too good to be true, it is. Second, after the conversation or call is over, I check out every claim. I don't care how reliable the source is. People lie, but they also boast, alter the facts a bit, and make mistakes. So listen, but listen skeptically, not credulously.

A Few Words on…Capturing Inspiration

The history of popular music is filled with songs that would never have happened if someone hadn't been listening. The members of Guns N' Roses were warming up for a gig at their condo in Los Angeles when guitarist Izzy Stradlin started playing chords. That led bassist Duff McKagan to improvise a bass line. Axl Rose, the singer, was upstairs but heard the music and started writing lyrics. The spur of the moment song became "Sweet Child of Mine." More? Well, in May of 1965, Rolling Stones guitarist Keith Richards woke up hearing a guitar riff, grabbed his guitar, and recorded the earworm. That became "(I Can't Get No) Satisfaction." And then there was Pete Townshend of The Who. He was writing songs for the rock opera Tommy, but an influential music critic was unimpressed. Improvising, Townshend asked the critic, "What if Tommy was a pinball champion?" The critic loved the idea, and the song "Pinball Wizard" was the result.

The lesson: Great, even life-changing ideas can come from subtle cues or fleeting moments. If you're not paying attention, you'll never know about the opportunity you missed. Be acutely aware of everything your customers say and do. If you're not sure if you heard something correctly, ask. Don't assume a remark was a throwaway or that an idea is too crazy. Seize the moment.

Salespeople are the True Artists

I've spoken with friends who are still in sales at Apple, and while they're thrilled with their stock options, they're frustrated that these days people still want to treat them as technicians. But that's not an Apple thing; that's a business thing. In big companies and small ones, leadership tends to treat sales as either a necessary evil or a process of going through the motions: making sales calls, inputting CRM data, writing orders, etc. And yes, it can be like that, but not when you're working with the best.

I would argue that in any great company, the salespeople are the true artists. Let's boldface that just to make sure you didn't miss it:

In any great company, the salespeople are the true artists.

Think about it. You're working without a net to manage the emotions and actions of other very smart human beings. You have to be in control of the encounter while letting the person you're listening to think they're in control. You're managing relationships and putting on a show and trying to win trust and doing it all with high stakes and a tangible goal: to get the other person to spend money. If you do it badly, you seem like a vulture. If you do it well, you can seem like a brilliant therapist—a trusted confidant and ally.

Great salespeople are artists and great listeners. That's what we had at Apple, and it helped that so many of us were musicians. I'd almost say that nobody should hire a salesperson who isn't a musician, but unfortunately, you'd get a lot of salespeople who don't wear shoes. No one wants that. So I'll suggest this: no company should hire a salesperson who doesn't at least have a strong appreciation for music. Because music lovers know how to listen.

How do you know if you're an artist or just a technician? Here's one way: does your selling hinge on *information asymmetry*? In other words, on you having information that your customer doesn't? If your entire advantage as a salesperson is, "I know what you don't," then you're coercing people, and that means you're just taking orders. If you're listening, understanding, and helping the customer write their story in a way that builds trust, you're an artist. Time to ask yourself which you want to be.

Michael's Excruciating Listening To-Do List:

- **Find good physical environments for listening**. This is basic. If you can't hear, you can't listen. Whether you're attending a meeting or sitting down with a customer, find a space where you can hear everything—sighs, chuckles, the other person shifting in their chair, everything. You never know what will tell you what you need to know.

- **Be present.** You can't listen if you're not mentally present. I can't tell you how many rehearsals or studio sessions I had where some of the musicians weren't present because they'd been out too late, their girlfriend broke up with them, or who knows what. It's disrespectful and a waste of everyone's time. When the time comes to listen to your team, your boss, or your customer, be fully present. Leave past issues and future concerns for later.

- **Determine whether you're profiting from information asymmetry.** Do you make a habit of concealing information from the customer that gives you an edge in negotiations? Or are you fully transparent about everything? If it's the former, I'd suggest you change things. The main reason is simple: eventually, your customer will learn what you've been hiding, and trust will be gone.

- **Practice.** You become a better listener by listening. I've already suggested listening to music with an ear for structure and how the instruments sound, but you can also practice listening in conversation. How well do you pick up people's names? Do you hear the meaning behind what's being said? Are you getting subtle humor and sarcasm the first time around? Can you relate back the details from the stories people tell you? Practice so-called "active listening," which in my book means listening without waiting for your turn to speak. Make listening and understanding your only goal in the moment.

- **Have some go-to questions**. It's always smart to arm yourself with great questions based on your knowledge of the customer and their organization, but you can also have a solid kit of go-to questions for any situation. Something like, "Tell me, what would you like to accomplish by working with my company?" breaks the ice and establishes a collaborative, caring tone. Write down and memorize some go-to questions that suit your personality and audience, and have them ready when you need them.

- **Take your ego out of it.** Finally, listening can be humbling when you hear something you don't want to hear. Leave your ego in your other suit when you sit down and remember that if your idea is quashed or you don't get the sale, it's not personal, no matter how personal it feels. Failure or rejection can be great lessons if you listen and know why they happened.

CHAPTER 4

Words

plural noun

\ 'wərdz \

A speech sound or series of speech sounds that symbolizes and communicates a meaning usually without being divisible into smaller units capable of independent use;

The entire set of linguistic forms produced by combining a single base with various inflectional elements without change in the part of speech elements

Examples:

Leonard Cohen, Joni Mitchell, Paul Simon, Tupac Shakur

You probably know the words to the song "Hallelujah," written by the late Leonard Cohen and covered by everyone from Jeff Buckley to Rufus Wainwright. They're gorgeous, evocative, and gut-wrenching—filled with images of pain, ecstasy, marble arches, and victory marches, and that lyric makes this one of the greatest popular songs ever written. Sure, the 12/8, gospel-inspired melody is moving and plaintive and beautiful, but what makes that song raise goosebumps is the lyrics—the words.

If the music is the medium, words are the message. A piece of music might put us in an emotional state where we're ready to receive a message, but the words *are* the message. They can be soulful, cutting and sardonic, seductive, funny, or any of one hundred other flavors of human expression, but what carries through is that the words always matter. They carry meaning in a way that music alone can't, and when you match the right emotionally electric poetry to the perfect combination of notes and rhythm, you get magic:

> *"There is a house in New Orleans they call the Rising Sun, and it's been the ruin of many a poor boy, and God, I know I'm one..."*

> *"Casey Jones, he died at the throttle, with the whistle in his hand, Casey Jones, he died at the throttle, but we'll all see Casey in the promised land."*

> *"Amazing Grace, How sweet the sound, that saved a wretch like me, I once was lost, but now am found, t'was blind but now I see..."*

> *"If Beale Street could talk, if Beale Street could talk, married men would have to take their beds and walk, except one or two, who never drink booze, and the blind man on the corner who sings the Beale Street Blues..."*

> *"He rocks in the treetops all day long, hoppin' and a-boppin' and singing his song, all the little birds on Jaybird Street love to hear the robin go tweet-tweet-tweet..."*

Lyrics can get under your skin, spark memories of your first kiss or best-ever road trip, bring tears of sorrow or joy—and you remember them for your whole life. Words are part of music, and they're part of any salesperson's artistry.

It seems obvious, but words mean things. They are precision instruments with incredible power. If you think I'm exaggerating, let me lay some names on you. *The Declaration of Independence. The*

Bible. The "I Have a Dream" speech. I could go on for a while, but I think you see my point. Words can change the world. They should be treated and used with respect. That's what we did at Apple.

I don't know how many companies have a Cambridge PhD in English in the marketing department, but we did. After Steve's return, we took words very seriously. The most obvious place you could see it was in our marketing, where we used brevity and careful word choices for maximum effectiveness. That continues today; Apple advertising and packaging are models of concise wit and impact.

Once I left Apple, I struggled with the startups I worked with because they were not using their words judiciously in their marketing. For instance, one company marketed to a higher education audience, but in their materials they would use the word "teachers." Well, in higher education, we don't have teachers. We have faculty or professors. It's a subtle difference, but when you're practicing the kind of listening we talked about in the last chapter, you can see it means everything. But the company didn't want to change the wording. Their reasoning (if you can call it that) was: "We don't want to invest in two separate marketing pieces."

I think my eyes are still rolling.

Like I said, words are precision instruments, and, like any precision instruments, they need to be deployed with care and customized for the audience you want them to influence. The idea that a company would let any kind of generic language go before its customers because it didn't want to spend a few extra bucks on marketing collateral is so completely at odds with what we learned at Apple that I feel compelled to share the most important lesson that we ever learned about words. Two words, to be specific. The two words that saved the company.

You already know what they are.

Think Different

The first thing you have to understand about Apple in those early days after Steve came back is that, despite the instant energy and hope he infused into the company, we were still living on the edge. Market share, sales...pick your metric; we were hurting. That wasn't going to be fixed overnight, but what did change was that Apple quickly became one of those legendary places that everybody thinks they understand while not really understanding it at all. You had to be there to know what it was like at Apple Computer (which was the name of the company when I started) to the day when Steve said, "We're are no longer a computer company. We're just Apple Incorporated."

When we asked him why the change, he said that the word "computer" was too limiting. There were too many words taking us away from our mission. He was already thinking five, six steps ahead of everyone else.

But before that came "Think Different." It was an advertising tsunami. It ushered in all the three-word "word-period-word-period-word-period" slogans you see in marketing today. But we were first, and none of them is as eloquent as "Think Different," and none of them encapsulates the soul of the brand like those two words did for us. Because we really did think different. We were like no other company—fearless, daring, ornery, ferociously imaginative, obsessive beyond belief, and musical. Always musical.

The only slogan that comes close is Nike's "Just do it," because, like "Think Different," it can mean a hundred different things to a hundred different people. You can attach your own significance to those phrases depending on who you are; that's what makes them great.

"Think Different" didn't come easy, though. Craig Tanimoto, the Art Director at Apple's ad agency, Chiat\Day, came up with the phrase in 1997, and Rob Siltanen and Ken Segall wrote the script for the famous TV commercial (along with input from lots of people at Chiat\Day and Apple). But before they got there—well, just put yourself in the room for a second with Steve, legendary ad man Lee Clow, and others. I wasn't there, but I can imagine what it must have been like, knowing Steve's driven personality and the trouble the company was in at that time, to keep turning over phrases and phrases, one after another.

It must have been hell.

I do know that Steve hated the initial TV script, but he kept going back to it and saying, "No, this will work. We need to do this." With that campaign, Steve was doing it again: taking somebody— even an advertising agency as successful as Chiat\Day—to a place that they had never been. Is that genius? Maybe. But that is definitely the difference between a leader and a manager. Steve wasn't waiting for someone to tell him what his vision was; he knew it. He was waiting to see if anyone else got it and could put it into words. Until then, he was going to keep whipping the creatives like Iditarod dogs and saying, "This isn't good enough. This doesn't encapsulate who we are."

Of course, to do that, you have to know exactly who you are, and Steve did. He knew exactly who he wanted Apple to be; the soul he wanted to fill the company. Talk about critical words! Every word the team chose forced out another word. They had to be perfect. Talking about writing under pressure...

Finally, they went with "Think Different." It was brilliant in its simplicity, and it was also a bit of a slap in the face to stodgy, boring IBM, which had its ThinkPad computer and the slogan, "Think." I never liked that campaign, because it seemed to be missing a word. More than that, when you tell me in a campaign, "Think," it sounds like you're presuming that I'm not thinking—that I'm stupid. To me, it always symbolized the arrogance and cluelessness of IBM.

In truth, "Think Different" was never really an anti-IBM thing. In all my years at Apple, we never perceived IBM to be an enemy. The original Macs ran on IBM's 68000 processors. IBM was never the problem. Microsoft was the problem. There was a true hatred for Microsoft within the company until they made the $100 million investment and made sure that Office would still be made for the Mac. I wasn't there, but I think in a moment of innovator-to-innovator gratitude, Bill Gates saved the company.

Anyway, the TV spot that Chiat\Day talked Steve into doing drove home how different we were from IBM and Microsoft in a way no TV ad ever has—except, maybe, for the famous "1984" Super Bowl ad that set the world on its ear. The script for the TV commercial was used nearly word-for-word based on what Tanimoto wrote. You probably remember it:

> *Here's to the crazy ones. The misfits. The rebels.*
> *The troublemakers. The round pegs in the square holes.*
> *The ones who see things differently. They're not fond of*
> *   rules.*
> *And they have no respect for the status quo.*
> *You can quote them, disagree with them, glorify or vilify*
> *   them.*
> *About the only thing you can't do is ignore them.*
> *Because they change things. They push the human race*
> *   forward.*
> *While some may see them as the crazy ones, we see ge-*
> *   nius.*
> *Because the people who are crazy enough to think*
> *they can change the world, are the ones who do.*[3]

Wow. I still get chills thinking about that, just like I do when I watch the TV spot with all those images of wonderful artists and geniuses who thought different, from Pablo Picasso to Albert Einstein to Gandhi to Maria Callas. And the world went crazy for the words. You have to understand something about the computer advertising of the time. It was all about speed and processing power and big monitors. Yet here's a computer company that makes silicon chips on motherboards, hard drives, and operating systems, and they haven't said a word about how fast or how much memory. To this day, Apple has not advertised what we used to

---

3   Hormby, Tom, "Think Different: The Ad Campaign that Restored Apple's Reputation," Low End Mac, August 10, 2013, lowendmac.com/2013/think-different-ad-campaign-restored-apples-reputation, retrieved May 9, 2019

call "speeds and feeds" in the sales trenches. That wasn't what we were about. As I said, Steve knew exactly what we were.

Apple was about the people, not the machine. That campaign was all about choosing words that made people feel like this was the company that would enable them to be what they'd always wanted to be—that respected the stories of the people who would be using the technology and wanted to lift them up and say, "This is for you. This is for you to be amazing. This is for you to do whatever you can do." Steve knew that, and once someone gave him the words that expressed that idea, he ran with it. Two words changed everything. Two words really did change the world.

Of course, not everyone got them. I'll never forget one of the first times I presented the new product concepts that the company was moving forward with to a faculty senate meeting. An English professor rose and said, "You do realize that 'Think Different' is grammatically incorrect."

It took every ounce of my self-control to suppress the innate Hageloh sarcasm, bat my eyelashes at her boyishly, and reply, "Why, yes, professor, I do." We heard from hundreds of people, some of them truly outraged, about how we were mongrelizing the language and making poor grammar cool. But other people, the truly creative ones, got our wordplay and understood what we were trying to say. We weren't just saying, "Think differently" with poor grammar.

If you dig down to the core idea of the slogan, there's a level of subtext with some missing words, and if you fill in the missing words, you get what we meant. This is the slogan with subtext added:

Think (about being/doing/living) Different.

The subtext turns those two words from an English teacher's nightmare into a manifesto for Apple users—a call to orient their minds on being different, being rebellious, being daring, and being like no one else. It was empowering—something driven home for me when I met with a member of the film studies faculty at the University of Florida. She wasn't a Mac user at the time, but she had one of the ad posters—the one with Gandhi—on her office wall. I was interested in converting her film program to non-linear editing on Final Cut Pro, and when I saw that she had the Gandhi poster, I asked her, "What does that mean to you?"

I'll never forget her answer. She looked at me and said, "Well, it kind of makes me feel like if I use Apple gear, I will be Gandhi." I said, "I don't know if I can promise you that, but we could surely make your films work better." But inside, I was cheering. That was exactly the effect we wanted the ad to have! To this day, though that professor is now in Missouri, she's still an Apple user. She loved the idea that Final Cut Pro would give her a different and personal way to tell the stories she wanted to tell through film.

"Think Different" was more than an advertising campaign for us. It was a culture. The greatest thing about Apple was that we thought different. That campaign wasn't about two words. It was about telling the world who we were. And God, did it work.

A Few Words on...Contrast

One of the reasons music and words go together so seamlessly is that both depend on contrast and texture to be effective. If you listen to a multi-movement piece of classical music, or even a rock suite like "Bohemian Rhapsody," you'll notice that each section is designed to contrast with the others, to either build on the feel of the previous part or play off it by being louder or quieter, faster or slower, more dense with notes or more sparse. Words work the same way both in a song and on their own. When you're speaking to a customer or making a presentation, you're probably at your best when you contrast information-dense explanation with moments when you slow down and ask the listener to think; or when you alternate thunderous sermonizing with quiet moments. Human beings respond best to the "delta," to a change in state—a new sound, tempo, or visual. The more you vary your tempo, volume, the density of your words, and the emotion in them, the more you'll engage your audience.

Eloquentia Perfecta

In music, words are called *lyrics*, and I like to think of lyrics, poetry, and similar forms of writing as *words with a purpose*. You might say, "Michael, don't all words have a purpose?" and I would ask you why you're talking to a book, which is an inanimate object. Get help. But no, not all words have a purpose. People often spit out words to make noise, fill space, or pretend they know more than they do. The entire field of sales training is built on the deployment of battalions of meaningless words that overwhelm by their sheer volume.

Lyrics have a purpose: to tell a story and evoke potent emotions in three minutes. If you can do it in fewer words, do it. In *Hamlet*, Shakespeare nailed it when he wrote, "Brevity is the soul of wit," but I think of words as the mixer in a cocktail. The more you add, the more you dilute the potency of the good stuff. That's why short form writing is so challenging and why the people who can do it well are masters. It's relatively easy to tell a story or get across a message when you have unlimited words, but your audience doesn't have unlimited time or patience. That's why "Think Different" was so miraculous. It captured Apple's identity and the aspirations of our fans in two words. That's the same reason I consider greeting cards to be one of the highest forms of poetry. Yes, they can be cheesy, but if you've ever seen a mom get tears in her eyes after reading fifty words written by some card writer at a desk at Hallmark, you don't doubt their power.

Making words work for you in sales means thinking like a lyricist or poet—using the right words, in the right combination, at the right time, and using exactly the number of words you need and no more. The number-one tool of selling is words. Words are the marketing department's primary tool, too, but the brilliant part of great selling is this ability to bring sales, marketing, and the customer together in a sort of Venn diagram. That lets the customer get a taste of a larger vision as he absorbs the messaging of marketing and your practical words about his needs and the new directions you can take him in.

Know what to say, know how to say it, and say it well. That's the Jesuit rhetorical art that I learned in school—the *Eloquentia Perfecta*. Nothing I've learned in life has served me better in my career.

The key to mastering this level of communication is speaking intentionally, becoming conscious of the words you choose to use in a particular context and, just as important, what words *not* to use. People who aren't in sales tend to throw language around recklessly, unaware (or unconcerned) about the impression their words are leaving behind, like leaves falling into wet concrete. But the best salespeople choose their words and their delivery deliberately. They don't speak to fill space but to leave an impression that serves their goal of connecting meaningfully with the customer.

Instead of small talk, they speak succinctly, making intelligent observations or asking good questions. They use words precisely, not relying on pop culture cliché or sales jargon. They're masterful at using pauses to let listeners absorb what they've said and respond thoughtfully. Maybe most importantly, they bury their ego. A great sales pro doesn't use language to show off his intelligence, name drop, or dazzle with his vocabulary. He leaves them like breadcrumbs, where they can reveal his character.

At Apple, when I called on someone, I was there to *communicate* the brand, not to *represent* it. There's a nuance there. Communication is two-way. The rhetorical arts are collaborative. You can argue with yourself, but it's no fun. That's where musicianship comes in. Go to a live concert and watch the audience. When the act is doing its job, the audience is alive, moving, and singing. They're not passive. They are communicating with the band as much as the band is communicating with them. That's why, if you talk with musicians or actors, they will tell you all about the energy that they draw from the audience. It's a real thing; I've felt it and fed off it. I've also done shows where the house was empty or dead, and each of my drumsticks felt as heavy as a bowling pin.

Communicating in a great sales meeting, when you're in sync and vibing off one another and the words come effortlessly, should deliver that same jolt of energy. If it doesn't, you're doing it wrong. Language exists to take your customer to a place, and when you get to that place, your products happen to be there.

Words have three functions in the context of *Eloquentia Perfecta*. The first is to *inform*. It's language as a teaching tool, sharing information. The next function is to *direct*, to tell people what they should do, in a sly manner that persuades but doesn't coerce. "Bill, what if you were to give a MacBook to every design student, so they could create incredible things anywhere, at any time, whenever inspiration strikes?" is compelling. "Bill, you should equip every incoming freshman with a MacBook" isn't. It feels like you're being sold.

The last function of language is to *evoke* emotion, and that's the most powerful one. When you have evocation combined with information, you get action. When you get people fired up to act and provide a compelling reason to do so, that's power. Sure, it can be used for evil as well as for good, as anyone who's been to ugly political rallies can tell you, but the tools are the tools. They work. Why do you think great political speechwriters are always in such high demand?

Steve brought with him an appreciation for *Eloquentia Perfecta* and a love of language. Before him, management wanted us to be conventional and robotic—more focused on how many calls we'd made and how long we'd spent on the phone than with engaging our customers' hearts and minds. God, they were clueless! Amelio, Sculley and the rest made us into ventriloquist dummies. Steve believed in taking talented individual contributors who were aware of the power of language and turning them loose. In other words, hand out the music and then let them play it with intention and emotion. That's what we did. Steve freed us to be artists. Again, that's leadership.

That new level of respect for words was probably the most dramatic change that I saw over my twenty-two years, particularly after the return of Steve and then again after he left as CEO. He passed away months after I left the company, but he had already been out of the business for a while because of his illness, and you could see the difference when the sales team got together as a group. The language used in our presentations was an afterthought; uninteresting. Common, boring sales words like "faster" and "harder." We didn't leave meetings feeling like we could leap tall buildings in a single bound. There was no inspiration, just perspiration.

Yes, words matter that much. They're nutrients for the mind and soul. Pre-Steve, our language diet was bland and boring, and it's no coincidence that our products were the same: forty-two versions of the same box trying to be everything to everybody. Instead of building one incredible thing and developing evocative marketing language that touched forty-two different people, we had to sell forty-two different versions of the *same* product and try to touch forty-two different people.

Touching forty-two of anything will tire you out, and that's all I'll say.

Writing Your Sales Song

There haven't been many songs about salesmen, but there have been a few. The Monkees recorded one back in 1967 called, creatively, "Salesman." Of course, if you look hard enough, you can find a song written about virtually any subject you can think of. Writing words and setting them to music is one of the most basic human activities, going all the way back to the sea shanties of Old World sailors, the ballads of medieval storytellers, the shamanic songs of indigenous peoples, and probably a lot farther.

What can you learn from lyrical composition that will help your selling or the sales department that you're leading? Plenty. Composing the words you'll use to engage, persuade, and inspire a customer isn't very different from composing the words a songwriter will use to woo a beautiful woman or get an audience singing along. It all follows a predictable pattern that I, though not a lyricist myself, will share with you. These are the parts of a lyric:

- **The intro.** If you listen to a great lyric like, say, the Beatles' "I Saw Her Standing There," it gets you into the world of the song immediately. Instantly, you know you're in the head of a boy looking at beautiful girl. Or take Wilson Pickett's classic "Mustang Sally." Right away, you know the singer's talking about a fast-driving woman who's probably trouble.

Great lyrics don't waste any time setting the scene with a few well-chosen words. In sales, your intro should set the scene for your customer—make it clear to the person on the other side of the desk that you know the current situation and what it means for them: "Evelyn, I heard that Arizona State just launched a new one gigabit wireless network on campus. Wow, I'll bet that's going to tempt some of your film and computer science faculty." That's an intro that leaves them ready for more.

- **The hook.** The hook in any song is its signature, the thing that keeps them coming back to listen again and again. The vocal "woo-woo" in "Sympathy for the Devil." The guitar lick in Tom Petty's "Breakdown." The flute solo in Jethro Tull's "Living in the Past." But words can also be hooks, like the "shake it like a Polaroid picture" line from Outkast's "Hey Ya!" The right words give the listener something to hold onto even after they've forgotten the rest of the song.

In selling, the hook is any phrase or line that grabs your listener's attention and stays with them. It's what they quote back to you the next time you call, or if you're really good, ten years later. One of my favorite hooks was from "I'll Take You There" by The Staple Singers. The song's funk beat is contagious, but it's that repeated "I'll take you there" line that grabs you.

In selling, a great hook is uniquely you, capturing your personality and style while knocking the listener down with its urgency, poetry, or truth. Think of it as your "mic drop" statement—the thing that, after you say it, leaves the room stunned.

• **The refrain.** You also know this as the chorus, the climax of the song that the singer goes back to again and again. It's often the only part of the song the audience knows the words to, and if they know it, boy, will they sing it. Think about the repeating line about the party being over at the heart of Prince's classic "1999." That's a refrain.

A refrain in sales is your go-to information, the true north that you always come back to. It's something that you need to keep reminding the customer about that has nothing to do with features, benefits, or price. You keep returning to it throughout your meetings.

• **The bridge.** If a typical song structure is ABABCAB, the C is the bridge, connecting the first part of the song to the verse (A) and refrain (B) that will finish it off. The bridge transitions us to the second half of the song, sets up the conclusion (sometimes through a key change) and creates tension and drama. For example, the bridge in the great Billy Joel song "New York State of Mind" is the part that talks about being out of touch and missing *The New York Times*, and then leads into the next verse and a sax solo.

The bridge is the connective tissue of your sales conversation, allowing you to move, for example, from imparting information to evoking emotion intended to move the customer to act. It's language that eases that move without being awkward and might rely on tactics like asking if the customer has questions, posing hypotheticals, or telling a story. Your bridge is like the side of a swimming pool: you should be able to push against it to move into the next stage of your encounter.

• **The coda.** A coda is a final tail on a song—the gong at the end of "Bohemian Rhapsody" or the endless piano chord at the finish of The Beatles' "A Day in the Life." It's a grace note intended to leave the listener with a certain feeling or impression.

Your coda might be an invitation to come to your office, a gift you hand over as you leave, an offer to create a personalized proposal, a promise to connect your customer with an important person, or nearly anything else that suits you and your style. What a good coda should always do is suggest further activity. *This isn't our last meeting. We'll talk again. I'll have my assistant set something up for next week.* It leaves your listener wanting more.

But once you have the words down, how do you deliver them in a way that delivers the greatest impact and puts your customer in a frame of mind to really engage with what you're saying? Well, I'm no singer, but I've worked with a lot of them, and the best ones knew how to do what vocal coaches call "writing the letter."

Too many pop singers focus their energy on the melody, mostly so they can hit the high notes that make everybody cheer. Sure, that's fun, but that's not singing. That's vocalizing, and vocalizing is just about sound. Singing is about emotion and storytelling and words. The words of a song are more than syllables you use to shape the sound—they're the soul and guts of the song. If you just run through a fancy vocal line but neglect the words, you might wow your listener, but you won't move them. If you want to move them the way that "Think Different" did, you have to write the letter.

That means expressing the words—the lyrics in a song or the lines in your sales pitch—with the full freight of emotion behind them and using them to tell a story with characters, drama, highs, and lows. Listen to great songs like Nina Simone singing "Love Me or Leave Me" or "Respect" by the great Aretha Franklin. There's loss, love, anger, pride, and humanity in those songs and thousands of others like them. You can imagine the lyricist writing those words in a letter to someone they love or someone who hurt them. You can feel the hope and pain.

Be aware of every word you use, the story you're telling, and the emotion attached to it. If you can do that, you'll go beyond selling to real connection.

An Annoying Musical Interlude

Ever since lyricists have been putting words to music, they've also been hiding hidden meanings in them or messing with listener's minds. For years, the classic party song "Louie, Louie" by The Kingsmen was alleged to have profane lyrics, when in reality, the only obscenity on the original record came when the drummer yelled "Fuck!" after dropping one of his sticks. The Sixpence None the Richer hit "There She Goes" is about a heroin high, not a woman. And John Lennon deliberately wrote the nonsensical words to the Beatles' "I Am the Walrus" (while on acid, he claimed) to mess with fans who obsessed over and often applied their own bizarre meanings to every Beatles' tune.

The lesson: If you don't make the meaning of your words crystal clear, people will hear what they want and interpret them in their own way, not how you want to them to. Choose your words carefully.

Big and Small Pictures

Most organizational leaders are not artists, but you'll need that kind of leader if you want to use words in this way. Because words are so commonplace, executives and managers easily overlook their power or misuse and waste them. Steve was a tortured artist—nothing more, nothing less. He had a lot in common with other great minds (including the ones featured in the "Think Different" TV spot): volatile, don't fit in, arrogant, audacious. I wonder if that's why Lee Clow chose those people for the ad, because they were like Steve?

People want to have their geniuses handed to them in an easy-to-digest form, and that's just not how it works. A musical organization comes at a price—usually, the death of a lot of norms and roles. If your marketing department isn't working out, find the tortured artists and put them in charge. I'll guarantee that out of the 200 people in there, there's someone toiling in anonymity who will change everything. After all, the guy who was responsible for the iPod was a mid-level manager.

To be an organization whose sales are inspiring, soaring, and passionate, you need people who can think around corners. You need an atmosphere that creates those heart-stopping moments when somebody suggests *The Idea*. You know what I mean: the idea that makes everybody in the room stop and stare at each other for a moment, knowing that you just hit the jackpot. That was "Think Different." To create that environment, you don't just need managers and salespeople and engineers. You need poets.

Under Steve, Apple gave us inspiring words, but they were all closely connected to the places that our products could take customers. My job was to take those words and bring them down to slightly more practical terms, because I was dealing with folks who loved to be transported but were also trying to get something done. The best words in selling are a mashup of soaring rhetoric and grounded reality.

So that's the blend. If you're a manager, you're responsible for the big-picture words that bring your salespeople into the fold, get them excited, and make them feel like part of the greater vision. If you're an individual contributor, you're responsible for distilling those words down to something that will suggest collaboration and value in a thirty-minute sit-down.

The trick is knowing which words to use when. Not long ago, I was talking with a fundraiser in the higher education space where I work now, and she was bitterly complaining that people who were out talking with donors were using big-picture metaphors when they should have been in their small-picture headspace: how the money would be used, what might be built with it, how that would impact students, and so on.

I understood her frustration. Context is critical. Not everyone is an artist, and even the customers who crave inspiration might not want to sit through an hour-long recitation of your company's vision if they're busy and stressed out. What they really want are practical solutions fast, so they can get to their next appointment.

Keep in mind that the effect of your words will be personalized. Each of us has a rich inner life and a history that others know little or nothing about. Even if you've been calling on a customer for fifteen years and they've become a friend, you're just skimming the surface of their inner life and how music (and words) might affect them. The first time I heard "Think Different," it hit me like a brick because I saw instantly that this wasn't just a command but something unique to each individual based on what thinking different meant to them: "Maybe if I got a Mac I would be Monet."

When you account for that in your sales, that's subtle, masterful selling. It means being hyper-aware and very adaptable. I'm going to talk about improvisation in Chapter Six, but when you lay your words on people and they react in a way you didn't expect, that's when you have to be quick on your feet.

I hate to blow my own horn, but—who am I kidding? I *love* to blow my own horn!—I was really good at thinking on my feet and adapting to how a customer reacted to my words. By the time Steve came back, I was kind of a legendary individual contributor. The term "classic Hageloh" became a thing at Apple. It was no accident. I had a blend of qualifications that made me perfect for Apple: I was a musician, I knew the academic world, and I loved the Apple brand. Selling Apple was easy for me.

Still, it isn't like you can go to the *Thesaurus* and just pick a different word. It's not about word choices. It's about the emotion you want to evoke. Two things bring out our primal emotions:

writing and music. When we started carving stuff on cave walls, those symbols meant something. They were words: *Don't go outside, there's a big thing out there that will eat you.*

You could be dealing with customer emotions that are just as primal. My suggestion: know how you'll pivot to a new rhetorical strategy if something you say lands with a thud. It's great to be able to improvise, but it's better not to have to.

A Few Words on...the Voice

Your voice is your instrument. Never thought of it that way? Most account executives haven't. That's why they don't take care of their voices or use them properly. Now is the time to start. Think of your voice as a finely-tuned instrument to be treated with care and used to deliver the words you've worked so hard to craft. There are three aspects of speech that you'll need to pay close attention to. Diction reflects how well you pronounce and enunciate your words. If you swallow your words or mumble, no one will understand what you're saying. Projection reflects how well you add sharpness and power to your voice so you can be heard by many people in a crowded room that absorbs sound. To project better, breathe deeply before you speak, and direct your voice through your nasal cavities and out the top of your skull. That will add brightness and clarity.

Pace reflects how quickly or slowly you speak. Our own voices always sound normal speed to us because we're used to them, but to others, you might sound like you're speaking unbearably fast. Consciously slow down, especially if you're nervous, until your voice sounds strangely slow to your ears. It will sound just right to your listeners.

How to Compose Your Lyrics

BE CONCISE

The most important rule in writing is Rule Seventeen from *The Elements of Style*, by William Strunk, Jr. and E.B. White. It says, "Omit needless words." In other words, start by writing out what you need to say and then ruthlessly cut every word that's not necessary.

KNOW THE AUDIENCE

One of the first things I did when preparing to see a new customer was doing the legwork to understand my audience. I always looked over the hierarchy, and if the person I was meeting with was at a senior level, I would adjust my language to be a little bit more formal. A few levels down, I might be a little bit more colloquial in my language. But at a senior level, I never talked about specifics or dollars. My talk was always about vision and emotion—how Apple would change the organization.

As you work your way down, become more practical. I became known for the phrase, "Don't worry about the numbers. If the products are right, we'll make the numbers work." We were twenty-five percent more expensive than Windows machines, and that phrase always disarmed cost concerns. That's the journey: making the customer crave what you can give them, then showing them how they can get it.

DON'T SELF-EDIT

The reason most writers don't finish anything is that they start thinking critically halfway through. Instead, put your head down and write out your pitch, presentation, report, collateral—whatever tool you need. Finish a first draft. Then edit, and be kind to yourself. First drafts of anything stink. Except for the first draft of this book. It was flawless.

USE KEY WORDS

You should know the language that's significant to your customers. Use those words liberally where appropriate in your compositions. For example, in my meetings with higher education decision makers, words like *partnership, outcomes, success, inspiration, Gatorade*, and *rhythm* proved to be hits inside and outside Apple. (Note: During our near-death days we had tchotchkes with a very unique "inside Apple" acronym on them: MIETDBWA—pronounced: "me et du bwa." It meant, "Making-It-Easier-To-Do-Business-With-Apple." Goofy, but effective.)

BE IRRESISTIBLE

When you take the lyrical approach, you won't need to ask for the sale, so don't. That breaks the spell. When I got really good at applying *Eloquentia Perfecta* to my selling at Apple, I never asked for the sale. I took customers on a journey they enjoyed so much that they didn't want it to end. You could say the business asked for me.

The Road to the Stage—Manager

You're the artist who needs to set the tone for the culture of words in your organization. Encourage your department and others to be more intentional in their language—in memos, reports, mission statements, you name it. Encourage account executives to read more and look at great marketing campaigns to figure out why the words work so well. If you have a soundtrack at the office, program it with music featuring rich, textured lyrics. Encourage outings to acoustic concerts where you can hear the words. Pay to send them to writing classes. This may sound ridiculous, but you're trying to help your people become captivated by the beauty and power of words. If you make your company a safe space for them to find their inner poet or bard, more than a few of them might surprise you.

The Road to the Stage—Individual Contributor

Learn about language—not just sales language but all language. Think about the words that bring forth strong emotions in you—things your dad said, something someone wrote
in a high school yearbook, favorite songs lyrics or poems.
What moves you to tears, makes you angry, or sparks powerful memories, and why? Try your hand at writing songs—I'm
serious. They don't have to be good, and you don't have to
show them to anyone. But writing in the ABABCAB form will
help you get a better idea of how words can be strung together to create potent meaning. If that's a bridge too far (pun
intended), then break down the lyrics in some of your favorite
tunes. Where are the parts of the song? What words are key
to evoking emotions? How can you apply that knowledge to
your selling?

Words Are Your Secret Weapon

Everything else we've talked about becomes real when it takes the
form of words. Words are your first point of contact with the customer like your tires are your car's point of contact with the road.
That's why knowing how to use them strategically is the secret to
Apple-like success.

Too many account executives still fall back on facts—spec
sheets; mechanicals. Maybe they're uncomfortable with emotion,
but in sales, emotion is your stock in trade. You lead with it nine-
ty-five percent of the time. Even in college fundraising, we're very
careful not to talk about the mechanics of a donation. Instead, we
talk about the big picture. What will the donation empower? What
will it foster? Word choice matters.

I'm a fan of melody, so I'm not a big proponent of rap and
hip-hop (or maybe I'm just an old guy), but when the words in a
rap song are on target, my God are they devastating. They have
to be like verbal razor blades to evoke emotions without melo-

dy to open the door. That's careful, strategic, self-aware use of language, and that's what salespeople need. Think like a rapper.

Seriously, break your lazy verbal habits. We did at Apple. One cardinal rule was no three-letter acronyms and no jargon. People still did it, but if Steve heard about it, it was not good. We also avoided clichés, which is good advice for songwriters too. Have you ever rolled your eyes at a lyric that used a hackneyed phrase like, "Baby, please don't go?" Customers do the same thing at oldies like "core competencies" and "ROI." Evict them from your vocabulary.

It's easy to roll out features and benefits and acronyms, answer objections, and just pitch. It's much more difficult to write lyrics that make an impact. That takes time. It takes pain. It takes putting yourself in your audience's skin. Find a way to know the dream that's haunted your customer for ten years. If you can help them realize that dream, you're golden. A salesperson's job is to be the bridge between people's crazy vision and the real-world experience they want to have.

Remember, Steve always insisted on not following the market, because the market will always take you to mediocrity. That's true both for products and the words you use to sell them. You don't create poetry by worrying about grammar. You get great by fiercely following the vision inside your head and praying it makes sense to somebody.

Michael's Excruciating Words To-Do List:

- **Read everything you can get your hands on**. Books, magazines, plays, poems; it doesn't matter. Get to know the different ways words can be put together to create meaning. Learn what combinations of words create warmth, disquiet, fear, etc. Write down the words you'd like to use in your presentations.

- **Study great marketing campaigns and terrible ones.** Marketing is the cousin of sales, and you can learn a lot from how copywriters and creative directors use words—or misuse them. Good marketing can provide a terrific example of how a few words can convey a world of meaning—a skill that's invaluable for any sales professional.

- **Get speech coaching.** If you're concerned about your diction or projection, get some coaching from a speech and language pathologist, or by attending some Toastmasters meetings. You might even consider taking singing lessons from a vocal coach. You'll learn how to project and also how to take better care of your vocal chords.

- **Use your phone.** There are plenty of apps that can help you become a lusty devourer of rich, wonderful words. For the iPhone, try *Word of the Day* app, which sends you cool new words to learn daily. For Android, try *A Word a Day Widget*, which does the same thing.

- **Go and hear people speak, and especially read poetry, in public.** You'll experience the power of the words and speech firsthand and see how it affects other people.

CHAPTER 5

Rhythm

noun

\ 'ri-_th_əm \

The aspect of music comprising all the elements (such as accent, meter, and tempo) that relate to forward movement

Examples:

Rush (Neil Peart), Cream (Ginger Baker), Led Zeppelin (John Bonham)

We've got our rehearsal routine. We've listened to each other play our distinctive riffs and started writing some lyrics. Now we start to dig into what makes sales flow like music. The heart of that is *rhythm.*

In the distant past (something most of us would probably define as the time before the availability of broadband), traveling salesmen would venture forth from Dallas into the small towns of North Texas, using miniature examples of their products to pitch the locals and get orders. They were known as "drummers." And if you think that's the source of the phrase "drumming up business," you're in the ballpark.

The phrase came into being during the Civil War, when peddlers in the South kept their wares in a box made of a wooden frame with a stretched leather cover. The tautness of the leather gave the box a sound like a snare drum, and when a salesman approached a farmhouse, he'd use that to announce his presence. He would grab a pair of sticks and start drumming on his box to let the owner know he was a harmless seller of goods—not a bad idea during the Civil War when tensions were high and an unannounced stranger might get a bullet between the eyes.

In other words, rhythm has always been a part of selling.

Q: What do you call a one-handed drummer?

A: A conductor.

Everything Has a Rhythm

The word *rhythm* originates from the Latin *rhythmus* and before that from the ancient Greek *rhuthmós*, meaning "any measured flow or movement." People want to be in a flow. They want to have a rhythm, to be working in unison, whether it's a fifty-person startup or a corporation of ten thousand. Everybody wants to feel they're a valued instrument in the orchestra, creating something beautiful while contributing to a grander vision.

You establish that through consensus, but someone has to lead the ensemble and make sure all elements of the music happen at the right time. That person is the conductor, the keeper of the beat. If you're managing a big sales department, you could be responsible for setting the rhythm for hundreds of people. If it's just you, then you're laying down your own beat.

It's easy to look at the conductor standing at the head of an orchestra and conclude that he's not really a musician. After all, he's just waving a stick, right? But he's keeping the beat, and by doing that he's determining when everything in the piece of music happens. That's essential. As science fiction writer Ray Cummings once wrote, "Time is nature's way of keeping everything from happening all at once." Without rhythm, music doesn't have a house to live in.

Imagine that you're listening to your favorite song—an oldie by Elvis Presley, hip-hop, maybe Bach—and instead of the verse/chorus progression you expect, or one movement leading into the next, everything happens at the same time. That's not music. That's cacophony. That's what I hear when I hear feral cats fighting—or when I'm forced to listen to jazz.

Everything is about timing, from comedy to sex. For us to get the results we want, things need to happen in a certain sequence and at a pace that feels right. We have to be attentive to the signals the other person is sending us so we know which passage to play at what time. What makes that precise timing possible is rhythm. The book you're reading right now has its own rhythm and timing, with one idea leading to the next and building on what's gone before. Without that, what I write wouldn't make any sense (and still might not).

In an orchestra, you might have seventy-five skilled, headstrong artists each bringing his or her own vision to a piece of music. The conductor uses the rhythm of that baton to bring everyone together, ensure that everything happens when it's supposed to, and lend a sense of order and control to activity that could—if let off its leash—career shockingly *out* of control. That's a pretty damned good description of a technology company. That's why the leader of a company needs to be the rhythmic heart of the organization—the conductor. During much of my twenty-two years at Apple, that conductor was, and could only be, Steve Jobs.

Steve Jobs, Master Conductor

Apple was known for breakthroughs, innovation, and doing and thinking different. We needed a strong heartbeat to keep the independent thinkers, harebrained ideas, and wild-ass geniuses on the same page, so at the end of the day we'd have something sellable.

That was Steve. He was our drummer, the keeper of our rhythm. It wasn't just that he was CEO; there was more to it.

Steve often came to speak to my team in Higher Education sales, and we could sense his love for the collegiate environment. That's why many of today's iOS products were launched—and debugged—in schools long before they enchanted the general public.

What made Steve a master conductor and keeper of rhythm was that he was always in total control whenever he spoke, whether it was to two people or two thousand. Remember that in Chapter One, I told you that Steve didn't just rehearse a speech; he walked through every detail of his presentation beforehand. When he stepped onstage in front of hundreds of education account executives, he knew precisely what he would say and do and at what pace. Steve played his people like a virtuoso.

But what's really fascinating is the fact that at this point in his speeches, Steve would depart from the conductor model. Most conductors keep their ensembles under ironclad control. But remember, Steve would open these meetings by asking, "Are there any questions?" You would think that he would immediately lose control of the room, but nothing could be further from the truth. Steve knew one of the secrets of rhythm:

A great drummer isn't actually *on* the beat, but 1/16 of a second *ahead* of it.

It takes the brain that long to process the compression of air that creates the sound of a drumbeat, feel time and tempo, and react to them. The drummer needs to be moving to the next beat even as the guitarist is strumming his chord and the bassist is plucking that bottom string. If he's doesn't, he'll wind up behind the beat and take the whole band down with him.

Steve was always ahead of the beat. You couldn't surprise him. One of my favorite instances of this took place during a sales meeting at the Santa Clara Marriott in California. Steve, as he usually did, opened things up by asking if there were questions. Usually, there weren't any, because we all knew that Steve was so smart and perceptive but so unconventional that a question was likely to explode in the asker's face. But this time, a young guy on my team rolled up to the mic while the rest of us were waving him off, and said, "Steve, we all get company cars, and there's no eco-friendly car on the list. Could we get an eco-friendly car on the list?"

Dead silence. Those of us in the know put our heads in our hands and waited for the axe to fall. We didn't have to wait long. Steve leaned back on his chair, then pulled the mic to his face and said, "You guys get company cars?" More dead silence. It took the division accounting guys months to justify the company car thing.

Lesson: *Don't ask rock stars questions.* You don't go up to Neil Peart of Rush and say, "Neil, would you explain to me how you do the double bass drum foot?" He's going to look at you like you just crawled out from under a rock. He can do it; you can't. That's why he's a rock star and you're not. If you were, you wouldn't have to ask.

A Few Words on...Syncopation

Syncopation is defined as "a disturbance or interruption of the regular flow of rhythm." It usually happens when the stresses in a beat fall somewhere you're not expecting. For example, in a typical song in 4/4 time, the stresses fall on beats one and three: "ONE, two, THREE, four." If you say it to yourself, you'll feel it. But if the beat falls on the count of two, the song can feel jagged and jumpy, something you hear a lot in jazz and reggae. In sales, syncopation refers to something that's unexpected but planned—something you bring to the table that turns the audience's expectations upside down. That's not improvisation; improvisation is spur-of-the-moment. When you syncopate your sales, you're changing your rhythm in a way that might make the customer feel surprised and a little uncomfortable, but that also makes you unforgettable.

Rhythm is About the Person, Not the Process

Rhythm and selling might seem to have little to do with each other. Let this ex-drummer set you straight. Rhythm is only irrelevant to sales if you're following the old, coercive, let's-out-discount-the-other-guys strategy—the one that doesn't work. If you're selling to breathing, feeling human beings, mastering rhythm might be the best thing you ever do for your commissions. However, there's a catch:

Rhythm is about what you do, not the products or services you're selling.

Of course, the idea that you're selling yourself—not software, graphic design services, or wireless bandwidth—isn't new. For decades, companies have been encouraging their account executives to see themselves as service providers. The trouble with this approach is that it just turns the salesperson into the product. The nature of a product (or service) is that it's pretty much the same no matter who the customer is. There might be some superficial customization—a sunroof here, a different app store interface there—but for the most part, the offering is the same for everyone. If you're walking into every prospect's office proclaiming that *you are the solution*, but all you're doing is reshuffling the same deck of cards you dealt to the last guy, you're still just pushing product.

Take any selling approach you like—personality-based, solutions-based, whatever corporate buzzword you're using this week—and each is a process. The problem with a process is that it's designed to produce a product. That's literally all it can do. *Process = product.*

Building your sales around rhythm makes you something more. Free of the constraints of sales approaches, programs, and processes, you can bring value through consultative selling. That is where humans have the ability to outshine simple commodity price and availability factors. When you're fully present—listening, watching body language, controlling the tempo and meter of the conversation while remaining keenly attentive to the beats the other people in the room are laying down—that's when you not only get to know the customer but you let them know *you.*

That's where trust starts. When you think of yourself as the drummer or conductor, you have the power to bring together divergent viewpoints under your rhythm and compose a valuable outcome for the customer.

Wait a second, you ask. *Doesn't being tied to a beat limit my creativity in the field and reduce my effectiveness?* No. Here's why. You're the drummer. You're laying down the rhythm everyone else is following. Your words and actions are somewhat restricted by your attack, meter, and tempo, but that's good. Rhythm lends structure to sales activities, controls them, and keeps them from veering off in unwanted directions.

Think about the Hollywood screenplay. If you're a screenwriter, you have to obey strict structural rules, or your script won't get produced. But within the structure, you're free to write something as sprawling as *Lawrence of Arabia* or as weird as *Swiss Army Man.* Selling with rhythm is the same. You have to keep to the beat, but within that framework, you can invent, brainstorm, and problem solve like a boss.

As a salesperson, your mastery of rhythm *creates* the right environment to produce a quantifiable, positive outcome. It's not about a room. You can take the environment with you and reproduce it anywhere. From the first beat, your mind should be open to magic, ingenuity, and the passion your customer feels about their business and its possibilities. It's only when you are open to the rhythm of the moment—of how you feel and what your customer is thinking—that magic can happen.

Personality-based selling? No such thing.

Solutions-based selling? A relic. Send it to a museum with my compliments.

Just as the rhythm section is the engine of every band, rhythm will be the foundation of every interaction you have, whether it's with longtime customers or new prospects. Now let's break it down, piece by piece.

The Three Components of Rhythm

Steve Jobs was preternaturally ahead of the beat all the time. A sales rock star is the same way. Sales artists understand that to make a sale happen, everything has to happen at a particular time, in a particular order, at a particular intensity, and at a particular speed. What's more, the time, order, intensity, and speed vary with each customer. It's the same in music.

When I was playing live, I couldn't drum the same way gig after gig. Sometimes, the room would be cavernous and echoing, and I'd have to back off. Other nights, the space might have acoustics deader than Anthony Weiner's political career (bah-DUM-bum), and I'd need to make my snare brighter and my hits sharper. There were nights when the band's energy was low, and I'd have to keep them moving with a smart tempo, while on other nights, everybody brought their A-game, and I could just keep the beat. You must find and establish a unique rhythm for every customer based on listening, learning, and knowing who they are.

At its core, rhythm consists of three key parts:

1. Attack—The attack is the first thing you do—how you initiate the interaction. It doesn't matter if it's a demo or a conversation over drinks, there's a right way and a wrong way to kick off a song or a sales conversation.

2. Meter—What happens in what order. This has a lot to do with the culture of your company and your customer. 4/4 time is conventional and corporate. 3/4 time is waltz time, conservative and old-fashioned. 5/4 time is Dave Brubeck and jazz, improvisational and daring. Which are you?

3. Tempo—How fast things happen. Should you send a proposal a few hours after your sit-down with the pros-

pect? Depends on the prospect and your relationship. Tempo is about *feel*—knowing when to speed up and when to back off.

Rhythm is the timing of when things happen in sales, a "feel" that's different for every salesperson and customer. It represents ebb and flow, on and off, loud and quiet, light and dark, Batman and Superman...you get the drift. Humans thrive on contrast, texture, and variety, on tension and resolution, and that's what rhythm is all about. Pay attention to attack, meter, and tempo in your sales process, and you'll develop your own approach that uses variations in timing and intensity, delayed gratification, and intuitive perception to infuse the sales experience with energy even as customers fall under your spell.

One of the things that makes rhythm challenging is that while we all possess our own personal rhythm, in a sales situation you've got to be in tune with the rhythm of the room. If you have a boardroom full of executives and there's a $100 million deal on the table, you can't be lost in your own personal time. You have to read the timing of the room and adapt to it. You have to be 1/16 of a second ahead of the next comment, the next "No," the next whatever. Your job is to keep everybody moving forward. Get into people's heads, anticipate the beats, and be ahead of the beat.

Let's dig into these a lot more.

Attack

Go and listen to a pre-2000s rock song. Seriously, go now. Not something synthesized and sampled to death, but something with a real drummer hammering real drums with sticks and sweat flying. Doors, Eagles, Nirvana, Rush, it doesn't matter. Go and listen to how the song starts, and then come back. I'll wait.

(Michael hums an aimless "waiting for the reader" tune...)

Hi! I was tempted to go on without you, but you're back. Now, what did you hear? If you listened closely, you probably noticed that the song didn't just begin with everybody playing on "1-2-3-4." It probably launched with a tight, sharp one-beat punch-and-release from the snare drum. Call it a fill, a riff, or whatever you like, but that's the attack. In rhythm sales, your attack is how you get onto the field of play.

Just as in a song, in sales your attack is how you initiate the action and take control of the rhythm from the start. The critical attack comes when you first meet the prospect, because that's when you make your first impression. Are you prepared to start strong? Small things can make all the difference. I've watched deals die, not because of bad timing or tempo, but because the attack was botched. One time, everyone went out to lunch after a great first meeting, but the account executive turned out to have horrifying table manners. You could feel the customer recoiling. Early in the relationship, your attack needs to be near-perfect.

But you'll have more than one attack, just as a guitarist might have one attack when he begins a song, another when he launches into a solo, and a third when he goes back to verse-verse-chorus. In a meeting with a customer, one attack will come when you open the conversation and take control. You might have a second attack after the customer finishes describing her problem. Do you follow up with questions? Cut right to the pitch? Pull out facts and figures? If you said, "That depends on the customer and our relationship, Michael," very good. Go to the head of the class.

I was just kidding. That's my chair. Go back and sit down.

A third attack might come at the end when you suggest next steps. Every attack sets the tone for the encounter, but your most important attack will come when you first get to know your customer. That attack will speak volumes about who you are, what you stand for, your values, and a lot more. That opening attack—the "three, four!" punch that opens the song, has to be honest, authentic, and uniquely you.

Your attack might be a mix of:

- How you dress
- What you bring to the meeting
- The words you choose
- Your sense of humor
- How you listen
- Body language
- How you engage physically (shaking hands, hugging)
- The information you share
- The volume of your voice

Heck, it can be practically anything! You're bringing your *je ne sais quoi* to the table. You're establishing an expectation of who you are, so you damn well had better be consistent from encounter to encounter. If you engineer your opening attack to make a great impression but it doesn't reflect the real you, your customer will know it the first time the mask slips. Sayonara, sale. You'll have obliterated all that trust you worked so hard to build.

Just be yourself.

Here's a secret nobody else will tell you: *Every attack starts as a guess.* Sure, over time you develop an instinct about how to approach different kinds of people, but when you don't know someone, you're fishing. Sometimes, you catch an old tire. Once, I created a thirty-one-page proposal for a very large academic bid, but we didn't win the business. When I got the proposal back, there were two commas in the proposal that were placed incorrectly. The comment from the prospect was basically, "If you could not take the time to check this for correct grammar and usage, we cannot do business with you." Ouch.

Well, excuse me for my ignorance of the Oxford comma! The point is, you can't always predict when an attack will lead to a beat that rocks the house or one that drags. So control what you can. Be genuine. Be confident. When in doubt, attack assertively and take charge. The best drummers don't wait for someone else to establish the beat; they *own* it. Everybody else in the band takes their cues from the guy with the sticks.

Meter

Meter is about timing—doing the right things at the right moment and doing them in the right order. If you know music, it's about more than the time signature—the 4/4 or 3/4 in the top left corner of a score. It's about rests, line breaks...everything. Meter determines when everything happens. I know that sounds trite, but often all you need to make an impact is to leave enough breathing room in between your notes to let the customer appreciate the tune you're playing. It isn't how fast you deliver your message or how much noise you make doing it. It's about delivering the right part of that message at precisely the right time.

Activity for its own sake is never the goal. Meter is an integral part of great selling because it tells you when to take specific actions. You've led with your attack, that highly personal part of yourself. Now you're in conversation, listening, present in the moment. But sales is goal oriented. The idea is to progress toward a positive outcome, whether that's an RFP, a signed contract, or a great first meeting. What comes next while you're deep in that conversation? Do you present data? Ask questions? Offer to conduct research? Go for the close? Until you have a sense of meter for each customer, you won't really know.

For me, the essence of meter is equidistance from the previous blow. When you're playing the drums, there has to be an equal space between the previous strike and the next. Too much space and things slow down; too little and they speed up. Either way, things start happening at the wrong time. You can feel it. It's the same with sales. Too many salespeople are in a hurry, chasing outcomes and jamming as much information into the engagement as fast as they can. That's fear talking. Remember, we thrive on variation, texture, and opposition. Let air into your selling, and let the tension rise and fall naturally.

Then there's *silence*, the most underused tool in the sales arsenal. If I could teach one skill to account executives, it would be to sit comfortably with a big, deep silence. Few people can do it; they babble to fill up the empty space. But it's a powerful tool. Think again of a musical piece and how potent the rests are. There's tension in that momentary silence that begs for resolution.

Do an experiment. Search YouTube and listen to tunes like The Doobie Brothers' "Long Train Running" or "Rosalita" by Bruce Springsteen. What's the most powerful moment in those songs? It's the break. Everything stops, including the rhythm, and there's just silence and the tension of waiting for the music to restart. Silence is a critical part of meter. The silence between drumbeats is part of the music, like the negative space in a painting. Leave a silence and let it fill up the space and it becomes expectant, vibrating with anticipation. Without silence and space, there's no music. Just one long note.

Silence leaves the other party at the mercy of their imagination. It's amazing the conclusions people will draw—how they will literally *sell themselves*—if you leave a big, thick silence in the room, then sit back in your chair with a smile and refuse to break it. In this day and age of constant communication, silence is mighty. It lends words, ideas, and emotions so much more meaning.

At Apple, we were experts at silence. There was a lot of silence about our new products. That was all part of the song. We knew to keep our mouths shut, and the company made it easy because they didn't tell us what the new products would look like or what they would do. Even I, a twenty-two-year employee, didn't get any special privileges. I saw the first iPod one day before the general public did. That was it. But the rumors! The excitement! Impossible without silence.

To become skilled with the meter of your selling, become adept at handling silence. Learn when to use it, break it, and extend it. Get a sense of what your customers are comfortable with—who likes product info early in a meeting and who wants a proposal and time to think about things. Learn about their tempers, likes and dislikes, how organized they are (or aren't), and more. Create dossiers with their preferences. That's composing.

An Annoying Musical Interlude

I love to see how music and rhythm affect people, and technology has made it so much easier to create moving musical experiences. A few years ago, I worked with a tech company that has this incredibly cool facial recognition software that's used in nightclubs to create an age-appropriate soundscape. A camera scans people as they come into a club, and an algorithm computes their age. The system determines the average age of the crowd and compiles a playlist from the years they were college age. If the average clubgoer that night was in college in 2005, they might hear Green Day and 50 Cent; if they were in college in 1990, they'd hear Madonna and Janet Jackson. People loved it.

The lesson: Music is personal. Sales should be too. If you can find a rhythm or storyline that affects your customer personally, that's a win.

Tempo

Tempo is the speed at which things happen. At pre-Steve Apple, our tempo had slowed down considerably. We became complacent. There's nothing wrong with a slower tempo—if it's intentional. But when a song starts to drag...oy.

A dragging tempo sucks the energy from a company. When I joined Apple, the tempo was at a rocking 150 beats a minute. But before long it started...to...drag. Before we knew it, we were down to 120. We'd started as punk rock, and now we were down to disco and still slowing. Before we knew it, we had completely lost our tempo. We were grinding. No one was ahead of the beat; we didn't even know what the beat was.

Technology became more and more pervasive, and we didn't even have an operating system strategy. We were actually using two different composing operating systems within the company! Can you imagine that now? There was no tempo for new products because we didn't have any new products. We did have Michael Dell, founder of Dell Computer, attacking us by saying, "They should sell the company and give the money back to the stockholders."

We heard the drumbeat of negativity every day. Apple's going out of business; Apple's done; Apple's this; Apple's that. Then, when Steve came back, he said we were going to invest ourselves out of this downturn, and overnight we picked up the tempo of what we were doing. We decided what kind of music we would play, stepped up the beat, built a new OS, and gained speed. It felt good. It took an infusion of Steve's energy—his ferocious drumming—to get us back up to 150 bpm and even faster.

In sales, tempo drives your meter and your attack. Of course, attack also establishes your tempo, so there's a cycle. But tempo determines more than the speed of what you do. It determines the energy, crispness, and freshness of what you give your customers. You click them in and give them the rhythm for what's to come, and then you roll out marketing, messaging, new products, updates, and beyond. Are all those components crisp, energetic, and sharp? Or are they behind the beat, outdated, and lagging? As any drummer can tell you, it's incredibly easy to let the beat slow down; it takes a single measure. You can't ever let up.

In the sales context, the most important part of your tempo is your *pipeline*. How many possible transactions are in it? How many did you close? Where are the opportunities coming from? Who are you talking to, how quickly are you talking to them, and what are you saying? A pipeline full of opportunities means a faster tempo, giving you more chances to talk to customers, build relationships, earn trust, and demonstrate value. To be clear, a full pipeline isn't the same as a lot of activity. There could be a lot of useless playing in your pipeline—mailing literature, walking the floor at a convention—that sort of thing. That's pointless activity, not fruitful action. You're the drummer for your own music. You're setting your own pace. If you set a slow one, everything you do will drag.

Think about how you feel when you have a day filled with stimulating activity and people. You might be busy from six in the morning until dinnertime, but it doesn't matter. You're keyed up, like a vibrating guitar string. That's what a crisp tempo does. Notice that I didn't say fast. I said *crisp*. The difference? It's a tempo where you're doing the right thing at a quick pace. There's intensity, but you're not rushing. You're not on the cymbals for the entire solo, making the dental fillings ache for everyone in the first three rows of the audience. You're moving quickly but with a purpose.

You've got your tempo dialed in if you feel engaged and charged up, if you're responsive to customer requests, if you don't spend your time racing deadlines, and if you're the first one to bring your customers new ideas, innovations, or solutions.

A Few Words on...Sticks

This is so obvious that I think a lot of people overlook it: drums don't play themselves. To produce sound, you must strike the head of a drum with something: drumsticks, brushes, brooms; your hands if you're playing congas or bongos. For simplicity, I'll call them all "sticks." The sound you get from the drum depends in part on the sticks you use. In sales, your sticks are the tools of your trade: sales literature, a PowerPoint presentation, a projector, a laptop, a proposal, etc. To get the best sound, you need to use the right sticks for the right music, and they should be of top quality. But the sticks aren't the music. I've seen account executives get so caught up in their tools—fooling with a laptop, reading off the stats from a spec sheet—that they forget to get into a rhythm. Remember this: *nobody* comes to a concert to see the drumsticks. They're just tools. Have them ready, but don't let them get in the way of being an artist.

How to Be a Conductor

I wish there was a set of easy-to-follow steps I could give you to make you into a master of attack, meter, and tempo. But there isn't. The reason is simple: rhythm is something you *feel*. When you're at a concert, out dancing, or just bopping along with a tune in your car, you're feeling the beat in your gut, tendons, and bones. There's no way to teach that. What I can do is help you understand how to create the right conditions to feel the rhythm that speaks to you—or, if you're a manager, your team.

SET A CLEAR BEAT EVERYONE CAN FOLLOW

In the early-to-mid 1990s, Apple was out of sync. We had more than forty different product lines. Every part of the organization was doing its own thing. We were like the "jazz odyssey" scene from *This is Spinal Tap*—a chaotic mess without the hilarity of watching Harry Shearer mugging in muttonchops. Marketing wasn't talking with sales. Sales wasn't talking to leadership. Leadership wasn't talking to anybody. If we'd died, it would have been a mercy killing.

When Steve came back, he had to lay down a new beat and get everyone else playing to it. That would've been a tall order for an engineer, but remember, Steve wasn't an engineer. He was a master storyteller. He knew that establishing a new beat for our products, messaging, sales, and marketing would run into a wall of resistance because people get comfortable with a rhythm even when it's the wrong one. So, after Steve took the CEO's chair, he killed all forty-one of our products in about five minutes.

At a companywide meeting, he announced our new strategy. "We're gonna do two things: consumer and professional," he said. I'll never forget the product manager in the back of the room who said, "But Steve, there are sixty product managers. What do you want us to focus on?"

Steve's reply: "Maybe your résumé."

Never question the rock star.

That extreme focus left a lot of bodies in its wake, but it gave us a sharp, clear new rhythm. By 1999, we'd cleared away all the product deadwood and rolled out the iMac and iBook for consumers, and the PowerBook and Power Mac for professional users like designers and musicians. We had our beat back. It's no coincidence that our next hit was the iPod.

You're not Steve Jobs, and you don't have to be. But in a company or on a sales team, there has to be one person through whom everything flows, who determines the rhythm. That person sets the tone for the entire group and makes it clear what's allowed and what's not. That might be you. That doesn't mean the first rhythm you set will be the right one; I can't count the number of times I messed up the beat of a tune in rehearsal. But someone has to take the baton and try to keep the beat. That's what a leader does.

If you're an individual contributor, then you're setting your own beat and have more room for experimentation. But that doesn't mean you should rely on someone else to be your drummer. If no one is conducting your entire company, find what feels right for you and stick to it. If you do have a strong organizational rhythm, try to integrate your beat into the larger one.

HAVE JUST ONE CONDUCTOR

I'm not suggesting that there's no place for artistic expression in your sales organization. Obviously, every individual is going to dance to a different rhythm, just like every player in an orchestra plays with his or her own unique flair. However, there's always one source of the rhythm, one goal everyone is working towards, whether that's creating the iPod or getting to the final note of *Rhapsody in Blue*. You need one person setting the tempo for sales.

Unfortunately, in my time trolling the startup world, I still see sales, marketing, and management teams where it's clearly every man for himself. There's no one setting a rhythm and making clear the benefits of following that beat. All they have is a disconnected bunch of soloists, not an ensemble.

Steve determined the rhythm of Apple. I was four people away from him, and every day I carried his message—not *my* message—into the business relationships I was building. We were his orchestra. I attended many executive briefings where we brought in all the different Apple departments. In those circumstances, with a room full of brilliant, headstrong, and creative people, you would expect everybody to just start talking at once. But not with Jobs on the drums. He didn't even need to be in the room; his authority as the conductor, the one whose vision kept us working toward what we all wanted, was absolute, and it kept everyone on the beat. Not out of fear, but because we knew following Steve made us and our company better.

Can this become dictatorial? You bet. Apple under Steve was *not* a democracy. But by giving us a rhythm to move to, he freed us to do great things. That's the price of having that single tight, clear beat. But someone has to lead. You can always fire the drummer and hire a new one. But somebody has to click the musicians in.

LISTEN

If you're an individual contributor, and no one is giving you a rhythm to follow, you're lucky. You get to set your own. In that case, open your mind and heart and listen. Pay attention to all the subtle cues in a meeting with a customer that most people overlook: the tone of voice, body language, their responses to your questions, the tension in their voice, how they enter and exit the room.... These are all clues to the particular rhythm you'll need to play to get that person moving in sync with you.

Also, listen not just to what people say but to the subtext. Why do they choose the words they use, and what does that say about them? For example, someone who uses words that suggest tension and stress in conversation might be under a lot of pressure in his or her job. Making the sale might mean easing off and adopting a slower, more relaxed tempo in what you're doing. The key here is that you, not the customer, should control the rhythm of the engagement.

FIND THE POCKET

You'll hear drummers talk about "being in the pocket" all the time. What do they mean? The pocket is that place where the tempo, dynamics, and feel are perfect for the particular song you're playing. Rhythm is about feel. Not only is the pocket for each song in your set different, but the pocket for a given song might change depending on how you and the other musicians are feeling that day, what the audience is like, and even the venue. The pocket for a thousand-seat arena isn't the same as the pocket for a tiny club that holds fifty people.

If you aspire to excellence, find your pocket—the rhythm that feels right for you. That's about your routine. It's how you get up in the morning. It's the calls you make. It's how you organize your day. All of that has a rhythm. Sales shouldn't be rote work. It's always different because the people and challenges are different. But if you want it to be invigorating, you have to bring your personal rhythm into it. You have to live with a rhythm.

Not just in your professional life. All the time.

Until he got sick, Steve had incredible energy every day. He was the human embodiment of Apple, and he didn't have a work persona and an "off the clock" persona. He was Apple and Apple was him. He knew his pocket and maintained that same rhythm every day, no matter where he was. What he did, what he was passionate about, what drove him each day—that's what made him who he was.

Once you discover your rhythm—your attack, meter, and tempo—lock it in. Find the pocket, and make that rhythm a part of who you are every day. But you also have to find something that you're passionate about selling. Without passion, you'll never find the pocket. Rhythm isn't a practice or a process or a method. It's a lifestyle.

The Road to the Stage—Manager

By this point in the journey to live performance, your company should be a confident ensemble with its own sound. But is everyone following the rhythm that you're setting down? You know they are if everybody in sales appears to be working toward the same goals, successfully collaborating. Tight, solid musical groups don't have one or two players straining against the beat that the drummer's giving them. If your team isn't in sync, you might not be giving them clear enough signals—which probably means the goals for the group aren't clear enough, or there's no single broad vision for the group that everyone can buy into. Start there. Once you address the big issues, you can work on the smaller details in rehearsal.

The Road to the Stage—Individual Contributor

I assume you work for a company and have someone else's beat to follow. By this point, it should be clear that being a strong member of the band means really listening, contributing ideas, and putting the team first when it comes to following the rhythm everyone else has agreed to. But as I've said, you can still make it your own. Follow your leader's big goals, but bring your own flair and style to the minutiae, like a drummer with his own bass pedal hit, touch on the cymbals, or way of tuning the snare drum. Push and push to bring your own individual rhythm to selling when you can, but be ready to pull back if you go too far.

We all sell. It's a deeply human activity. We might sell products, ideas and concepts, or take our peers and customers on a journey with the stories we tell them. We convince our families and friends to help us do things we care about. Asking someone out is selling. Getting that person to marry you is selling. Becoming president is selling. There's a rhythm to all of this, and if you can find the joy in it, it will become easy.

Great professional salespeople know their inner rhythm. They are hyperaware of their surroundings and themselves. They pick up on the smallest of details. They read the signals. Their minds work at one hundred and seventy-five beats per minute. They live every aspect of their lives with the same intensity and passion. Cultivate this ability and you will make good things happen.

Rhythm should be, quite simply, *who you are.*

Michael's Excruciating Rhythm To-Do List:

- **Develop your "anticipatory thinking."** If you want to be ahead of the beat, you have to be thinking several steps ahead of the customer, anticipating his needs. Think about what Apple did with the iPhone: we loaded it with dozens of subtle features and functions that fly below the radar...but when someone finds one of them, it feels like the engineers were reading their minds. That's being ahead of the beat. That's what makes everyone else follow you.

- **Maintain your rhythm when you go home.** Don't take it off like a coat. Bring the same purposeful, joyful beat to your relationships, workouts, recreation...everything. Set a comfortable tempo and maintain it.

- **Make sheet music.** Great drummers might look like they're winging it on stage, but that's only because they've been staring at charts or notes about how to play each song until their eyes hurt. Keeping time is the most structured part of playing music; you have to be precise. That means taking notes and dissecting everything you did to figure out how you can improve.

- **Fine-tune your drums.** Unless you're the CEO, you're going to be playing to somebody else's baton. But that doesn't mean you can't make the drums sound unique to you. Did you know that drummers tune their drumheads? It's true. Each head plays a note when you strike it, and that note has to be in tune. This is the perfect spot for a tension metaphor, so here goes. The tension in the drummer's drumheads is like the productive tension between smart, driven salespeople and smart managers. It makes music. A little tension and creative disagreement is a healthy thing.

- **Have fun.** Rhythm, dancing—they're pure joy. Find that in your work. When I was working with a startup called littleBits, we had Sonos players all over the office. But I grew tired of some of the playlists, so I suggested that every Friday a different person should build a playlist for the office. That was fun for me, and my Disco Friday raised lots of eyebrows among the twenty-somethings. One individual said, "You listen to this? Do you go to therapy?"

I have no idea if she found another job...

CHAPTER 6
Improvisation

noun

| *im-ˌprä-və-ˈzā-shən* |

The act or art of improvising

Examples:

Charlie Parker (sax), Charlie Musselwhite (harmonica), Jimi Hendrix (guitar)

My greatest closes came when things changed on a dime, and I was able to turn it around by thinking on my feet in the moment. Similarly, some of the greatest moments in the history of music were created in the moment: Jimmy Page on guitar in Led Zeppelin's "Stairway to Heaven," Neil Peart on drums in Rush's "Tom Sawyer," Ronnie Ross on saxophone in Lou Reed's "Walk on the Wild Side" and, of course, Jimi Hendrix's scorching rendition of "The Star Spangled Banner" on guitar at Woodstock.

I'm not comparing myself to Jimi Hendrix, and heaven knows not to Neil Peart, but I'm very much comparing the ability of great sales professionals to the ability of musicians to improvise soaring solos on the fly. As I've said, the greatest sales training I ever took wasn't meant to be sales training. It was an improvisational theatre class, and I think it was filler because the sales training we were supposed to get didn't show up.

If you've ever watched *Whose Line Is It, Anyway?* you know about improv theatre. There aren't any lines or characters. The person running the improv or someone in the audience suggests a scenario—say, two people standing on the window ledge of a skyscraper—and the actors make up the scene as they go. It's a high-wire act that's got a fair amount in common with performing a musical solo in front of an audience.

In one scenario, you stand up knowing that you're going to be making your lines and character up in the moment. In the other, you might know the song and have a chord progression in mind, but you're still creating something spontaneously. No two solos are exactly alike, no matter what the instrument is. You have to be open to what's happening around you and fearless about your choices, and once you play your first note or riff, you're committed. You have to see the improvisation through to its conclusion.

The improvisation that occurs during selling is exactly like playing a drum or guitar solo in front of five hundred screaming people. You might go into the arena with a plan and think you're prepped for anything that could happen—you've anticipated objections and have answers for them all, and you've got a rock-solid pitch—and then you get a curveball. Suddenly, the song you thought you were going to play has to change. You've got to let go of your plan but still apply everything you know, all your artistry, to get the conversation back on track and keep the customer engaged and feeling positive about you. Like everything else about sales, it's part training and preparation, part skill and creativity.

The best improvisation isn't actually improvised at all:

There are rules, approaches, and strategies that should guide you even when you're changing things in real time, and the best musicians and sales professionals learn, master, and use them.

So, let's take a closer look at the importance of improvisation in selling the Apple way.

Controlled Freedom

I've told you how tightly controlled everything was around marketing and messaging within Apple, and that's true. We didn't tie our shoes a different way without approval from Steve Jobs. But there was a big difference between the overarching corporate culture and what we were allowed to do day-to-day as individual account executives. To belabor the point (something I'm very good at), you can compare it to a sax solo in jazz. I don't like jazz because I'm a fan of melody, and jazz sounds chaotic and un-melodic to my ears, but it's the perfect genre of music to capture the idea of "controlled freedom."

If you listen to a recording of Charlie Parker or Miles Davis playing a solo on a tune like "Hot House" or "Freddie Freeloader," you might think you're hearing a chaotic mess of random noise (or, as jazz sounds to me, two cats mating in an alley), but if you listen closely, there's structure underneath. No matter how far the soloist strays from the line of the song and from the chords in the original key, he always comes home to that line, led there by the rock-solid notes of the piano and bass. It's freedom with control.

Even though Steve controlled every aspect of Apple's corporate culture, we had great freedom to be ourselves when we were out in the field with customers. Steve was our rhythm section—our piano and bass line playing in the background. But we never needed to check in with anyone or file reports. Steve and the other senior executives knew that because the reborn Apple was about aspiration and emotion, we had to talk to people from the heart—not from some prescribed sales system—or we wouldn't get anywhere. Remember, this was the time before the iPod and iPhone; even after the candy-colored iMac G3s came out in 1998, we were still selling hard into the education market. The era of "Don't Apple products sell themselves?" hadn't begun yet, not that it ever truly existed.

My problem with sales training to this day is that it imposes structure on something that can't be structured: human interaction. Sales training programs are security blankets for people who either don't have the talent to be in sales or lack the guts to be themselves and the work ethic to learn about their customers and connect with them in ways that matter. Sales "solutions" teach account executives not to think. *Follow the method,* they whisper, *and you'll close the sale.* And that's absolute garbage.

Once again, this marks the difference between leaders and managers. Managers spend hundreds of thousands of dollars on sales training programs because it's a blanket solution that lets them tell their bosses, "Yes, everyone's been trained." For the most part, managers are number crunchers. Very few great salespeople go into management; generally, they stay in sales. They know how organic selling is; you can't stamp out the process of creating re-lationships and reaching agreement with other human beings like it's a product on an assembly line.

Leaders, on the other hand, don't need a false sense of secu-rity. They know that sometimes, the best thing you can do is set up some guardrails and then turn your people loose. The guy who set up the sales training that ended up being a theater class was a leader who had a professional acting background. He brought to the table a brand of interaction with the customer that wasn't systemic. If you teach your account executives a system and the engagement goes in an unexpected direction, they're stuck. They end up babbling, right? System-selling robs you of your ability to think on your feet. Improvisation grows it.

But the worst part about system-selling is that it drains all the authenticity out of the encounter. You know what it's like when you're on the phone with a customer support person, and you know they're just walking through a question-and-answer tree? If this, then that, right? You don't feel heard or respected. That's terrible for building a relationship with your prospect, and today, when they can know as much as you do about your product and price, authenticity is your killer app.

Great account executives need the ability to turn on a dime and sense the moment. To do that, you have to be in the moment, not thinking "What comes next in the script?" And yes, actors work from scripts, but acting is not the same as selling for one simple reason: you always know what the other character is going to say. Even if you're acting in a play, where you don't have the luxury of shouting "Cut!" and doing another take like you do if you're making a film, you still know what the other person is going to say. That gives you, the actor, the freedom to memorize your lines, fully inhabit the character, and then be in the moment and react to the scene with genuine emotion. Knowing what the other actors will say is comforting. Salespeople don't have that luxury. We always have to be on the balls of our feet, ready to move in any direction.

I've been told that I have a face made for radio, so I've never done any acting, but I know from speaking and being a radio host that the ability to make an authentic connection to the audience, even if it's an audience of one, is a must-have skill. In fact, great speakers, radio hosts, and actors are great at making each person in the theater or the listening audience feel like they are an audience of one—like they're speaking directly to them. The best salespeople have the same ability. They can make you feel like your needs are the only ones that matter.

That doesn't happen in your typical sales training. In fact, most of them are painfully clueless. I had one at Adobe I'll never forget. They brought in an enterprise sales trainer, and I said, "We're in the education market. Our enterprise doesn't work like that." He smirked and replied, "All enterprises work like that."

Okay, you smug punk, it's on. In case you don't know the education market, it's its own animal. If you're running a department and you get a grant, you don't need anyone's approval to spend it. You can use it however you like. I said, "No, you don't seem to understand. My customers have their own money. They won a grant. Nobody can tell them how to spend it. It's their money. These are academics. That's just not the way it works." But this clown just could not get it through his head. He said, "Well, somebody has to approve it."

Sigh. There are few times in life when it's okay to condescend to idiots without fear of reprisal, and this was one of them. I was going to savor it. "You don't seem to understand. When a department head gets a grant for his research, he doesn't answer to anyone for how he spends it. There's him, and then there's God. That's why I call on them, because they can spend money on our products and not have to worry about any university standards."

The guy just never got it. He had no ability to think outside his tiny box. Actually, when he summarized that training session, he complained that I was disruptive in class. But I needed to be disruptive, because his class was idiotic. It was an enterprise selling course that the company had paid for; nobody cared about who the audience was. It was checking the boxes. "Yes, we've trained our sales team." But have you?

Canned sales approaches actually disrespect the salesperson, because they implicitly say, "We don't trust you when you're out of our sight." As esoteric as it might seem, the concept of this book—paralleling sales and live music—makes a lot more sense than the idea of dumping your sales staff in a pot, adding a selling system, pouring in water, and assuming you'll end up with something that grows. You're more likely to wind up with a group of men and women who resent you for wasting their time and treating them like children. We're artists, not Sea Monkeys (again, google it).

A Few Words on...Rules

Musical solos might feel improvisational, and to some degree they are, but they're also rooted in a set of rules that the guitarist, drummer, saxophone player, or harmonica player knows and follows. For example, structure. Any solo follows the structure of the underlying song, playing over the chorus and bridge chords, the verse and chorus chords, or something else that everyone agrees on. Also, no matter how far he strays from it, the soloist has to come back to the foundational key of the song. If the song is in E, the guitarist knows he needs to end his solo on a note that blends with that key. In selling, we have rules to lean on too. They might vary by the organization and even by the account executive, but we still rely on them to keep us on course. For example, one of your rules might be that you never talk about technical specs: "speeds and feeds" as we used to say at Apple. So, if you're in your pitch and the conversation starts veering toward specs, you know to steer in a different direction. Or maybe your rule is that you have a set of probing questions that you ask every prospect. No matter how the conversation begins and what rabbit holes you go down, you continue to navigate toward those questions, which always work for you. Improv? Sure, but with guardrails.

Maps Versus GPS

When I talk with people about improvisation versus systems in selling, I often use the metaphor of GPS versus using a map when you're on a road trip. GPS has become a critical part of our lives—not just in finding our way somewhere, but in everything from location-based services like Yelp to ride-hailing services like Uber. I can't overstate the value of GPS in driving the new economy, but it's crippled our ability to think for ourselves and on the fly. How many video clips have you laughed at that show some hapless soul driving right into a lake or river because they were blindly following the instructions of a GPS navigation system that was having a stroke? That kind of tragicomedy is only possible when someone abdicates their responsibility to think for themselves and becomes a drone following instructions without question.

I've known people who were spectacularly bad at following directions, but while they might wind up in a bad neighborhood or in the middle of a cornfield, not one of them ever drove into a lake when they were using a map. The deficit of GPS is that while it's incredible at giving you turn-by-turn directions to a destination, you don't have any cause to pull back and see the larger route you're on. You're not forced to make any decisions. When you take a road trip using a map, you're asked to make judgments and best guesses, plot your course, and think ahead. You can see the lake or river fifty miles before you get there, so you know not to turn down what is obviously a boat launch ramp because some female computer voice tells you to.

GPS is the equivalent of selling based on a scripted system. When you're selling according to Michael's Magical Musical Method (I won't call it by the acronym "MMMM" because it would sound like I just ate a brownie), you're using a map or one of those long-extinct Thomas Brothers map books that used to be standard equipment in car-centric cities. With GPS, you're not thinking for yourself. With a map, you can get a big-picture view of the prospect, the situation, and the progress of the conversation. To really torture the analogy, you can adjust your route as the road conditions change.

That's how sales went at Apple. On one memorable occasion, I was meeting with a customer, and the context of his history and current situation gave me a feeling in the pit of my stomach: *This isn't the time to make the sale. Say no and walk away.* So, I said, "You know what, I'm wrong. I don't think our products are a good fit for you right now." The guy looked at me like I'd just told him I was going to sprout wings and fly to Mars.

"What, are you kidding me? I've got $200,000 to spend, and you're telling me you don't want to sell me this stuff?" I said no. If I had been following GPS, the turn-by-turn directions would have said, "Say yes and give him the contract." I would have been thinking only about the outcome, because when you're following GPS, that's what you do. You lose any sense of the value of the journey. But I was using a map, so I trusted my instincts and improvised. I said, "No, I don't think this is right for you right now."

As you know if you're in sales, saying "no" to business is powerful stuff. It immediately says to the customer that you care about their well-being, not just their dollars. It's instant authenticity and credibility. In this case, the customer was deeply impressed and grateful that I was so honest with him. Two years later, he called me, ready to buy. But the deal had grown from $200,000 to $5 million. I'd increased the value of the sale by a factor of twenty-five by trusting my gut and improvising. Not bad.

By the way, when self-driving cars finally become viable transportation options instead of threats to pedestrians, this problem is going to get a lot worse. At least when you're using GPS you're still driving. With autonomous vehicles, we'll be breeding a nation of passive passengers who can't find their way home from the store, kind of like smart phones have caused us to forget the phone numbers of even our closest relatives. Instead, I refuse to trust any vehicle that doesn't lay on its horn and give me the finger when I cut it off in traffic. I'll take the surly predictability of the average New York driver over computerized comfort, thank you very much.

The Power of No...

Improvising, thinking for yourself, trusting your instincts instead of some out-of-the-box sales system—it all frees you to be yourself, not whatever management thinks a successful salesperson acts like. But one of the most important things about following a map instead of handing the wheel over to GPS is that you're allowed to leverage the incredible power of the word "no."

Earlier, we talked about the power of silence. Great salespeople know when to stop talking and let a pause spin itself out until the other guy buckles and breaks the silence. Well, as I mentioned when I told the story of walking away from a sure $200,000 sale, the word no has the same kind of power because it defies the customer's expectations. The implied social contract of the buyer and the seller suggests that:

1. *The seller will do whatever is necessary to make the buyer happy.*
2. *The seller will say yes when the buyer offers to buy.*

If you've ever been sucked into a deathly boring sales training, the decision tree or "if/then" algorithm always leads you to the same place: agreement. As Alec Baldwin barks in the film version of *Glengarry Glen Ross*, "Get them to sign on the line which is dotted!"[4] The only goal is closing the deal in the moment—nuance, trust, a bad fit, or the relationship be damned. A sales formula will not let you say no to money. That's a terrible thing when you're working in today's economy, where the customer has access to all the data you have and more buying choices than at any time in history. You're begging to ruin a relationship that might be years in the making. Some of the worst clients I've ever had were the ones where I knew it wasn't going to be a good fit but said, "No, I'll make it work."

On the other hand, when you're improvising, you're always reading the room, gauging the customer's situation, and making predictions about the future. You're free to say, "No," or "That's not a good fit," or "I don't think it's in your best interest to buy from me right now" when the moment warrants it. When you do, you can feel the energy in the room change. In a few words, you've turned the customer's expectations upside down. What started (in their mind, anyway) as a purely transactional meeting has instantly become something else. You're being honest. You're putting the customer's welfare ahead of your commission. Some of the best long-term customers I ever had were people I said no to—sometimes, more than once.

You can't say no unless you're free to, and you're only free to if you're free to think for yourself and make choices in the moment based on your instincts and experience.

...and Yes

Now that I've held court on the virtues of saying no, there's also a lot of power in saying "yes," at least when you think about selling in terms of improvisation. When I took that improv class from the University of Florida, one of the most important lessons was

---

4   Tokofsky, Jerry, Zupnik, Stanley R. *Glengarry Glen Ross,* theatrical. Directed by James Foley. New York: New Line Cinema, 1992.

that your response to everything other actors say is always, "Yes, and..." When you're trying to create something on the fly, saying no brings everything to a dead stop. It kills the scene by leaving the other actors nowhere to go.

But when you say "Yes, and..." you inevitably follow that with a new direction or character. It isn't always the right one; sometimes, the scene ends up a mess that has to be put out of its misery. But you create an opening for new possibility, and that means something good can happen, even if it doesn't always.

You're probably familiar with the idea of saying "Yes" in selling, too. The idea that saying no brings conversation to a halt is part of the standard sales vocabulary. I'm here to tell you why, and it's not because it's your job to say yes to what the customer wants so you can get a signature. As I said, sometimes saying no is your best weapon. No, the key improvisational phrase in sales is not "Yes, and..." It's "Yes, but..."

Why? Because "Yes, but..." is a *pivot phrase.* It lets you keep the conversation going but take it in a new direction. Unlike with improv theater, where your job is to build uncritically on what the other actor just gave you without having a destination in mind, in sales you're trying to take the customer to a destination. Using those words lets you acknowledge what the person has said—and avoid stopping the exchange dead in its tracks—while giving you a jumping off point for inserting a fresh idea or a different perspective.

That was kind of the way we ran things internally at Apple. There was always an acknowledgement of an idea, followed by something that took it in another direction. The one exception was Steve, who wouldn't shy away from telling you that an idea didn't work and wouldn't soften the blow with "and" or "but." That was just how he was. But even with customers, such blunt feedback often led to something no one had ever thought of, and that's where the gold was.

An Annoying Musical Interlude

Going into 1969, The Grateful Dead were just another hippie band from San Francisco's Haight-Ashbury district whose records didn't sell very well. The album that turned them into legends with a generation-spanning cult following was "Live/ Dead," and it was largely improvised. Recorded while playing live on January 26 at San Francisco's Avalon Ballroom and at the famous Fillmore West on February 27 and March 2, the Dead proceeded to spontaneously create the form now known as "jam rock," handing off lines and weaving in new textures with now-famous songs like "Dark Star." The result wasn't clean, tight, or even that technically strong, but those were never the forte of Captain Trips and the guys. The Dead were all about the feel of being there, and nothing captured that better than this improvised classic.

The lesson: Trust yourself. Rehearsal is important, but don't let it stall your creativity. If you're feeling the flow in a sales situation, go with it. You never know when you might create some-thing incredible.

What Goes into a Jam Session or Improv

As you've probably picked up on by now, I'm not a fan of the typical sales training that companies impose on their account executives. It stifles creativity and energy in the same way that designing a drum solo sucks the life out of it. I've played plenty of solos, and the best ones came when I was submerged in the flow and texture of the music around me.

I'm a big proponent of the concept of *flow* as articulated by psychologist Mihaly Csikszentmihalyi[5] (pronounced, "Ow! I think I just dislocated my jaw!"). That's the state where you're completely absorbed in and effortlessly focused on an activity to the point

---

5   Csikszentmihalyi, Mihaly, *Flow: The Psychology of Optimal Experience*. New York: Harper & Row, 1990

where you lose all track of time. Salespeople rarely talk about flow, but that's usually because reaching such a sublime mental place is impossible if you're walking through some prepackaged sales program. If you can let that programming go and follow your instincts, you can get into that "zone" where storytelling seems to flow off your tongue and persuasion becomes...easy.

What I'm really talking about in this chapter is *jamming*: not just soloing but spontaneously creating something new in real time according to the vibe of the moment, like the Grateful Dead. Businesses (including yours, if you're managing a sales department) can get a lot more mileage out of respecting the individuality of their sales force and combining that respect with work that focuses on developing the following abilities:

LISTENING

There's a reason I already devoted a whole chapter to listening. You can't improvise in a way that fits into a larger whole unless you're listening to what's going on around you. Improv actors have to listen to their fellow actors for cues and ideas on where to take the scene next. Musicians playing solos or jamming have to listen to what the other members of the band are doing so they can build on it, do a call-and-response, or create something new. Salespeople have to listen to what the customer says—and doesn't say—in order to know where the conversation should go next.

Many account executives aren't good at listening. It's like they worry that if they're not talking, they've lost control of the meeting, and it might veer in a direction that doesn't serve their interests. But you're not there to serve your interests; you're there to serve the client's interests, and the more you're aware of the timbre and rhythm of what's being said, the more you can shape where the conversation goes. Speak less. Listen more.

HOME

Jam sessions may seem free-form, but they're really not. If you've ever been to a concert where the band turned a four-minute song into a twenty-minute side trip of traded solos, key modulation, and wild exploration, you might have noticed that under it all, they always had the bass and drums keeping the tempo and the "bottom"—the chord progression of the original key. The band always comes home to that original starting point before rocketing off into psychedelic space again. Under every good jam and improv, there's a foundational structure: verse-chorus-verse, set-up-punchline, and so on. That's the good ones, mind you. The bad ones are chaos.

Sales is no different. You'll feel braver and more in control if there's a general structure to every encounter with a customer, a "home" that you can always come back to no matter where the conversation goes. For me, it was usually how Apple's products could help further the college or university department's mission, whether that was giving film students the best possible tools or aiding laboratory research. I could always come back to that home base as a way of keeping the conversation moving forward, but I could do it organically so it didn't seem forced and "salesy."

CALLING THE "SCENE"

Few things are more awkward than an improv theater scene that's going nowhere, but the actors insist on beating the dead horse. (For all the attention it's received in the last three years, *Saturday Night Live* still does this a lot.) That's why improvs almost always end with someone in the cast shouting, "Scene!" meaning that sketch is over—time to move on. Grateful applause. It's the same with a musical solo. A two-minute free-form adventure on the mandolin is novel and cool; a ten-minute one has the audience rolling its eyes and shouting, "Get on with it!"

It's important to know when to cut an improv, a solo, or the direction of a sales chat short—to stop before things get weird rather than wait until everyone feels uncomfortable. That's why sales professionals listen so acutely, so we can develop that sense that tells us when it's time for us to take the wheel and steer the meeting in a new direction. Work on developing your inner ability to know when to shout "Scene!" and then find the nerve to do it. It's your meeting. That's how you control it.

DESTINATION

Every jam session has a goal: to wind down side roads and narrow paths with the music, creating variations and new visions in the moment, but then to come back to the original tune at the end. When that happens, there's a palpable release of tension. We're home. We've been wandering in the wilderness of suspended ninth chords and spoken word poetry, but now we're safe. No matter how much groovy creativity you bring to a sales presentation, always have a clear destination in mind for that meeting. Is it to close? To get the next meeting up the ladder? To relationship-build? It's your job to bring the customer home and help them feel safe.

A Few Words on...the "Handoff"

Most jam session tunes follow a simple three-chord structure. For example, I played a lot of blues in my sordid past, and blues follows a classic twelve-bar structure called a "one-four-five." The main theme of the song lasts for twelve measures and only features the first, fourth, and fifth chords in the key. Listen to any old-school blues tune and you'll hear it. At some point when you're improving, soloing, or jamming, you're going to have to "hand off" the tune either to another soloist or to the ensemble. But you'll only do that successfully if you're paying attention to where you are in the progression of the song, so you can make the handoff at a place that makes sense. You don't hand off to the band in the ninth bar of your blues progression unless you want everyone to stop playing and stare at you. In sales, the handoff happens when you either throw the conversation to someone else in the room—probably the customer but possibly a partner—or take up the conversation. That's a critical spot, because you want to maintain the beat, but to do that, you've got to be mindful of where you are in the song: what's been said, how it's been received, where the emotions in the room are, and so on. Don't get lost in your own words, let your mind wander, or be thinking so far ahead that you lose track of the now. There's nothing worse than having your bandmate look at you and shout, "Take it!" and you're standing there going, "Huh?" Don't be that guy.

Round Tables

When Steve took the reins again in 1997, one of the first things he did was take all the rectangular tables out of Cafe Mac and replace them all with round tables. He did that so there could be more cross-conversation from people who didn't know each other. If I'm not mistaken, he did the same thing at Pixar. He also put the cafeteria in the center of company HQ to bring everybody together.

I bring this up because improvisation and jamming doesn't just occur in front of an audience or customer. Sometimes, it happens behind the scenes. Some of the best music my bandmates and I created came when one of us said, "Hey, listen to this!" in rehearsal and then rolled out a wicked guitar riff or bass line that the rest of us could build on. Some of the best sales ideas we had at Apple came when we were sitting in meetings talking about strategies and brainstorming with no filter.

You or your team might be at your best when you're in an unscripted meeting with other departments. We have all kinds of names for that now: mind mapping, idea generation, and so on. Most organizations have a culture of sitting and working on our own, which isn't conducive to creativity. But a hopeful and growing trend is for common spaces with a common white board where people can be doing their thing but can invite other people in to play and share their ideas. This kind of cross-pollination is why products like Slack do so well: they break down the traditional walls.

Apple had that collaborative, "let's put on a show" spirit long before it was popular. Sure, we had separate departments for education sales and enterprise sales, and it wasn't like the sales team was over in engineering helping design motherboards, but we were all sort of ricocheting around in this big creative playground, like electrons in an atom, encouraged to share and improvise. Steve and the leadership appreciated the fact that great ideas can come from anywhere—and often do. There were no walls between sales and engineering, software, or any other pieces of the puzzle. We were a part of everything that went on in the company.

You probably know that the iPod was sort of a mashup of ideas from a bunch of different sources: Toshiba and Braun and Bang & Olufsen, leavened with a blinding hatred of the big, clunky, awful form factors of the digital music players of the day. But it was true improvisational skunkworks collaboration between geniuses like Steve, Jon Rubinstein, and Jony Ive that made the iPod a thing and led to leaps like the iPhone. Is there any reason why sales and marketing can't collaborate with that same sort of unfettered brilliance and energy?

I don't think there is. Despite the widespread perception that we're just order-takers, sales is a dynamic, creative field. More to the point, no one is closer to your customers and how they use your products or services than your field sales force. If anyone can give you reports from the front lines on the innovations that customers are begging for, or the changes in current offerings that would make things better for your customers (and your bottom line), it's the men and women who are with the customers almost every day. My suggestion? Open your company culture up to open collaboration and improvisational thinking whenever you can. Include everybody, not just the "traditional" creative occupations like design and marketing. Encourage wild brainstorms and impossible ideas.

Remember what the "Think Different" ad said about the people crazy enough to think they can change the world being the ones who do? Those people wouldn't have gotten anywhere if they hadn't had someone to listen to them. Be sure your organization is listening.

Why Sales Systems Really Don't Work

Sales systems and sales training programs stink. Have you picked up on that? Good. I hope so, because I'd be worried about you if you hadn't. But before we close out this chapter, let's you and me dig into the real reason they don't work, because it's not what you might think.

First of all, let's have a reality check. I'm not naïve. You and I know that in a sales culture, the top line goal is making your number. That's critical. At Apple, we weren't there just for love and hugs. In sales, you're measured by your numbers, which is a much tougher metric than, say, engineering or marketing, where there's room for failure. So, when you're performing at your best and your company is hamstringing you with bad service or poor product, selling can feel like the hardest job in the world.

For example, I did the first-ever one-computer-per-student sale in the country, selling eight hundred of the old white iBooks to a college. But the product failed. It was embarrassing as hell for me, and it reminded me of the old joke where the doctor says, "The surgery was a success, but the patient died." Sometimes in this business, you make your number and still lose.

Other times, you don't make your number because you should never make your number at the cost of the relationship. It will take you twice as long to get a new customer as it will to keep the ones you already have. We treat sales like it's a solo act, but it's not. We're dependent on every other aspect of the business to do our jobs, and sometimes we crush it, but the band lets us down. I don't care if you're Etsy, Facebook, Apple, or Dell. Who's on stage with you matters, and to get the results you want, you may need to have your hands in departments that don't directly involve selling because your work depends on them being handled correctly.

For instance, at one point we were overloaded with iMacs that no-body wanted because they were not the best they could be. The command was, "We've got to sell these, no matter what." Well, I'm not going to destroy my customer relationships by giving them subpar products for the sake of moving inventory. It's not going to happen. Plenty of other account executives also refused to hustle our customers by pushing those computers, and they were right to do so. Was the quality of those iMacs my business? No. Except that it was.

Sales training doesn't work because it's only good for teaching the basics: how to manage your day, make sales calls, log contacts, update your CRM, and so on. None of that will make you anything more than an order-taker. The point is that you can't teach someone to be a great salesperson any more than you can teach a by-the-numbers rhythm guitarist how to solo like Eddie Van Halen. It's something you learn over time by doing—by tapping into your inner artist—and not everyone can do it.

That's the mistake many companies make. They think they can convert foot soldiers into masters. They think their system will be the difference-maker. That's like believing that a personal training system like P90X will make you a professional athlete. It might get you fitter and make you look better, but without athleticism, that's it. There's nothing wrong with that, except that when we apply "anyone can do it" thinking to sales, we create unfair expectations.

Everybody thinks they're a salesperson, and in fact very few people are. Everybody thinks they're a writer, and few people are. Everybody thinks they're a soloist, and few people are. Holding tight to your self-delusion is harmless until it affects your livelihood, or other people's. A culture that believes salespeople just take orders creates a situation where salespeople don't see our own value—a culture where Gil Amelio can say, "These things sell themselves, just get out of the way." Well, Gil almost bankrupted the company, so I guess they weren't selling themselves, were they?

At Apple, we had people like me who had the temperament for dealing with academics and understood how to work with Stanford, with UC Berkeley; with UCLA. We had a strategic initiatives team that I was a part of late in my career, and we were the people who debuted the ideas that became consumer products later on. Every one of Apple's early major consumer successes was tested first on campus. Why? Because we knew how they thought in higher education. We knew that on campus, where thinking is open and people get excited about disruptive new ideas, they would be open to trying out innovations and tolerant of failures. Experimentation and bold failure are the university stock in trade.

Who provided those insights? Sales did. It's one thing to walk around campus, but it's another thing to recognize the possibilities for not only the education customer but for the rest of the company. The best sales professionals can do that. The reps with the confidence to improvise and play solos are the ones who learn about people and themselves, test their ideas, push back against the restriction of their roles, and see themselves as creative artists. You don't train those people. If you're very lucky, you find them and give them an instrument to play.

The Road to the Stage—Manager

When we talk of improvisation and jam sessions, that's where the drummer metaphor becomes most relevant. It's also where a lot of managers start to sweat. On one hand, you're the consistent, reliable beat going on while all your creative salespeople and marketing types are riffing, soloing, and going off on wild-ass tangents. It's your job to keep them focused on the larger goals, maintain discipline, and so on. But that can also be nervous time, because as a manager, you probably find disorder...well, disorderly. It makes you nervous. Letting your sales force too far off the leash is scary, because what if they go off the reservation, and you get blamed? The only thing I can say about that is this: it's not your job to rein them in. They're adults and professionals. It is your job to give them room to play, discover, and stretch while keeping them safe. The best VPs of sales I ever worked with erred on the side of giving their people more freedom, not less, and trusting them. That's how you break through goals.

The Road to the Stage—Individual Contributor

Right now, you're probably not ready to launch into a four-minute solo jazz exploration, and that's fine. I wouldn't expect you to be. We've barely made the transition from talking about the mechanical parts of playing live music—rhythm and words and rehearsal and all that—to the more "feel" aspects like improvisation and soul. We'll get to more of that. Right now, it all feels a bit alien, I suspect. So, all I can say is this: trust yourself. When Steve came back to Apple, the greatest gift he gave each of us was to let us know we could trust ourselves as creative individuals again. No longer would we be shouted down, ignored, or marginalized because we had an idea that went against the corporate grain. It was our job to go against the grain, and that included us in sales. When we all trusted ourselves, good things happened. No musician can play a solo without trusting that in the moment his fingers or mouth will know what to do and he'll be able to come up with something beautiful. Trust yourself. The rest will come with time and practice.

How to Hold Your Own Jam Session

SOLOS, NOT SILOS

The improvisation and collaboration I've been talking about in this chapter can't happen in an organization where departments live in silos and fiercely defend their fiefdoms. Do a Steve: tear down the walls and replace the rectangular tables with round ones. The most productive sales environments are the ones where sales is mixing it up with marketing, engineering, operations, and more—

trading solos, sharing ideas, and developing that jam session vibe that can only happen when people work face-to-face.

GIVE EVERYBODY THEIR STAGE TIME

Not everyone is a natural soloist or jam player. However, I've seen some reluctant, skittish musicians blossom in an improvisational setting when given the chance to experiment on stage without worrying about being told to stop. The smartest thing any leader can do is spot someone talented and give them a venue to discover and develop those talents. That's the stage. In sales, that means letting gifted reps test their ideas for pitching and closing customers without imposing systems on them. It means allowing inexperienced people to learn from the veterans, not from boxed programs. It means giving salespeople air and space to create and mess up, within reason. Sometimes, the cost of developing a world-class sales pro is a few lost contracts.

MAINTAIN A CONSISTENT BACKBEAT

During a serious jam session that might go twenty minutes or more, the drummer is usually the one keeping the train on the tracks by laying down a consistent backbeat. In the corporate setting, that backbeat is your culture, values, policies, or mission statement—the rock that the sales force can come back to when they're uncertain about what's acceptable or how much to concede to a customer. If a desirable customer wants a big price break for a huge order, is that policy or do you stand firm on pricing? We rarely discounted at Apple once Steve came back because, like Disney World, we didn't have to. Keep that backbeat strong and clear, and if you're in the field, listen to it.

PLAY YOUR WAY

One of the main reasons I hate sales training is that it bleeds the personal style out of account executives and turns them into robots. If you're field personnel, you're not pushing product, you're trying to relate to human beings—so be yourself. Play the kind of music that lights you up. If you're funny, be funny. If you're a storyteller, tell stories. If you're concise and to the point, great. And if you're selling for an organization that won't let you be who you are, find a new one.

When to Follow the Music

All that said, my years at Apple showed me that there's also a time when you should *not* be improvising and, instead, stick to the music. Steve Jobs micromanaged virtually everything at Apple, and while individual improvisation was a powerful force, behind the scenes was always that iron control of the message and language. The two are compatible...if you manage them the right way.

Apple was very collegial. Most of us had the equivalent of tenure, which in academia means that you can chart your own path, within constraints. There were underlying rules, and within those rules we had a great deal of freedom, but if we strayed outside of those boundaries, we heard about it.

For example, as long as I stuck to the approved messaging and sold the Apple brand as Steve and the powers that be had conceived it, I was free to chase any opportunity I thought might be fruitful and take lots of chances. Believe me, I chased many an opportunity that turned out to be a big zero. That was okay, because many times it *didn't* turn out to be a zero. In sales and in other areas of the company, as long as your risk-taking yielded some successes, you were encouraged to have some failures too.

That opened up a lot of creativity that had been bottled up in our old traditional corporate structure, in which failure was career death. Three strikes, you were out. So, you didn't solo. You played nice, safe chords. It wasn't an environment where breakthroughs happened.

The trick is to maintain a hard wall between the public side and the internal side of the organization. Think about my world—the university. A university is made up of various colleges that run themselves, but everything ultimately runs through the dean. Each college might have its own culture and methods, but the dean and the culture he or she dictates is the public face of the university. There are some common underpinnings, but a college of art and sciences is not a college of business is not a college of medicine. Yet they all operate within the same structure and mission set by the leadership.

Steve was the dean of Apple, and as much as he let us be *Animal House* internally, externally he exercised absolute control. We weren't allowed to solo once we stepped outside the door. That's why secrecy around new product releases was so perfect. The goal was to get massive amounts of earned media coverage (which we did), and you didn't dare jeopardize that. Mr. Jobs was a showman like few other CEOs have ever been. He knew that the best jam session is worthless if the concert isn't masterfully stage-managed.

Leaders know when to maintain control and let their players improv. Great salespeople know when to toe the line and when to step into the spotlight and let 'er rip. If you have both, you've got something special.

Michael's Excruciating Improvisation To-Do List:

- **Create a safe space for "dumb" ideas.** Stupid, impossible ideas were our stock-in-trade at Apple. They should be yours, too. You have no idea when a sales tactic or prospect group that seems ridiculous will pay off. My maxim is "Everything is impossible until somebody does it." Create a safe space on your team or in your department for your reps or colleagues to suggest the absurd and ridiculous. Reward them for it. Encourage them to test their ideas and be proud of brave disasters...kind of like Chicago's "Hot Streets" album. Ugh.

- **Offer multiple channels for communication, and then let it happen**. Improv and collaborative magic take place when people communicate, and while that's easy in the rehearsal space or studio, it's not always easy in an office. Trouble is, managers make the problem worse by trying to dictate how their reps connect. Instead, set up multiple channels—in person, messaging, meetings, whatever—and let your people decide how they'll communicate.

- **Don't be afraid to dump what doesn't work.** Some sonic adventures don't pan out. Some solos or new chord ideas flop. Good bands leave them on the studio floor and move on. If you try out a new sales approach or test a new market and the results aren't great and you can't figure out what went wrong, don't be too timid to cut bait. There are always more ideas.

- **Don't get so caught up in the solos that you forget the basics.** I can't tell you how many shows I played and saw where the talent of the musicians was undercut by bad amps, faulty mics, lights that didn't work, or one of a hundred other screwups. It's great if you're feeling creatively daring, but don't forget to attend to the basics—or, if you're a VP of sales, give your reps the essentials. Talent won't make up for missing or outdated collateral, laptops or projectors that don't work, or even something as simple as a bad phone number.

- **Tune up.** In 1981, I signed into a War cover band. "Low Rider" was one of my best grooves, and I was looking forward to playing it. But one thing I learned in the music business was that while everyone touted their credits, credits don't replace talent. Our Anglo lead singer was full of credits where he had played, but he was completely off-key and didn't have the chops to sing "Low Rider." His previous bands hadn't mentioned it. We fired him and got a Baptist preacher who had no credits but all the groove in the world. Credit is nice, but nobody ever signed a deal with a résumé.

CHAPTER 7

Soul

noun

| *'sōl* |

The moral and emotional nature of human beings;

a strong positive feeling (as of intense sensitivity and emotional fervor)

Examples:

Aretha Franklin, Janis Joplin, James Brown

In 2010, I launched my political career. It lasted for one election, which I lost. But the launch taught me something about soul, which is that you can't fake it. The radio show I hosted ("The Michael Hageloh Show," how's that for an original name?) on WOKF in Florida reached tens of thousands of listeners, but what everyone called in about was my theme music. "Who was it? Where did it come from? Who's the artist?" Really? It was Barry White's "Love's Theme." These people didn't know Barry White! Most of them had probably been conceived during one of his song's. Long story short, even though this was 2010, and the song had originally been recorded in the 1970s, it was an instant retro-hit. That's proof that soul transcends time to connect with people. Apple was built on those deep connections.

Now join me in the present day, and I'll make that story relevant. Not long ago, I spent three days with fundraisers from all the community colleges in Texas. It was the kind of party you think of when you think "college fundraising": strippers, a Roman orgy, cage fighting, you name it. All kidding aside, they brought in a speaker who spent nine years as the lead fundraiser for Yeshiva University in New York. That's the school where you send your son or daughter to be a doctor, even if they drool on themselves a lot.

At one point, Yeshiva had their entire endowment invested with this guy by the name of Bernie Madoff. When things fell apart, they were gutted. Lost hundreds of millions of dollars. But there was a woman there who consults with schools all over the country about fundraising, and she told me that by helping Yeshiva secure just four new donors, she had not only helped the school recover from the Madoff disaster but doubled the size of its endowment. She's very good at speaking, but not because she gives her audiences lots of content. She's charming and funny and engaging, and donors seem to respond because of her humanity.

During her speech, one of her key points was that fundraising is marketing. Being successful at it means bringing people to the point where they buy into you as a human being. Once they do that, you can get them to buy into the institution. Not only do I agree, I've seen the same thing happen so often that you'd think more organizations would have figured it out by now. After all, there's a saying in sales and marketing that's so old I think it predates the wheel: "People don't care how much you know until they know how much you care." It's stuck around this long because it's true.

This takes us back to that eternal tension between leaders and managers. Managers want to make all things predictable and repeatable, and in some cases, that's good. In a corporation, you want things like your finances to run like a finely tuned machine. The trouble comes when you try to apply that same mechanical approach to things that are inherently messy and human, like sales. It doesn't work. You suck the humanity—the *soul*—out of the process and actually hurt outcomes.

I was able to close nearly one billion dollars in sales at Apple primarily because my customers felt connected to me personally. They knew me and cared about me, and they knew that I cared about them. Remember, during most of the 1990s, Apple was not the juggernaut you know today. We were a fringe player, completely overshadowed by Microsoft and always on the verge of going out of business. I can't tell you how many times I heard, "Michael, I'd love to buy this from you, but I don't know if the company's going to make it."

Despite the uncertainty, my customers often bought...because it was me. They weren't doing me a favor (nobody spends $5 million because they like my dimples—except my wife, but that's a story that should be told over drinks); they trusted me when I said that Apple was going to make it through the hard times. It's the same in fundraising. Donors don't always understand where their money is going when they write a big check. They're writing it because they like the story I'm telling, and they trust me personally.

Nothing can replace that personal connection and the emotion, passion, and empathy that come with it. That's especially true in the technology world, where there's so much distance from people and everyone's always trying to engineer the human being out of the process, presumably because people are expensive and unpredictable. The moment you hear that your company needs fewer salespeople, assume you're going to want more of them. Assume you'll need better salespeople—not cheap, poorly trained ones. When the other guys are cutting back their sales forces, you should be building yours into a trust machine. That's your edge. It was one of the factors that brought Apple back. When Steve took over and we started building things that people wanted again, we already had those relationships.

A Few Words on...Call and Response

Call and response is one of the classic parts of soul music. It's where one musician—say, the lead guitarist—plays a phrase, and then one of the other musicians on stage—

say, the organist—picks it up and copies it, often with some embellishment. C&R is a fun feature of soul songs that can repeat over and over as long as the audience and players enjoy it. In sales, "call and response" has nothing to do with sales calls. Instead, it's about delivering an emotional message that resonates with your customer and letting the customer feed that message back to you with his own touches added. For example, you use carefully chosen words to paint a picture of what your customer's company could look like with your product—a picture you know strikes an emotional chord. Now you have your customer seeing and feeling what the future could be—and hopefully, making that vision his own with some embellishments. As long as your ideas are authentic and you're not trying to manipulate the customer, this is a great way to get buy-in for ideas that will benefit everyone involved in the transaction.

What is Soul?

By this point in the book, you should be pretty well-versed in the mechanics of creating music—arranging your rehearsal, writing your lyrics, telling your story, establishing and keeping a strong rhythm, and all the rest. It's all very important. But know this:

Technical mastery doesn't equal music. Making music takes soul.

You can know the notes, but you still won't be the King's Singers or the Harlem Gospel Choir. By the same token, if you've ever seen a jam band like the Grateful Dead or Phish live, you know that technical skill isn't really their forte. What separates mechanically skilled studio musicians from the artists who set the stage on fire or make congregations weep and sing is feel, emotion, energy, passion—*soul*.

Think about some of the greatest soul musicians in history, legends like James Brown, Etta James, Aretha Franklin, Marvin Gaye, Amy Winehouse, Ray Charles, and the aforementioned Barry White. Think about what made them great. Yes, they were technically brilliant artists, but that's not what gets you dancing and swaying and singing along, even today. It's the heart, vulnerability, and honesty of their music that affects us most. When you hear Etta James sing "At Last," you can *feel* her joy at finding her true love. When Aretha belts out "Respect," and tells her man how he needs to treat her, you want to stand up and shout, "You go, girl!" because you can *feel* her pride and fierceness. That's what I mean by soul.

In sales and in business in general, soul means showing up as a human being who shows emotion, is vulnerable and real, and cares about not only the customer but people in general. That's becoming more important, mostly thanks to the millennials and Generation Z, who seem to be unwilling to accept a world where business and commerce are soulless. In 2018, a strategic intelligence firm called Department26 polled one thousand millennials about their relationship with work and found that they cared more about passion and infusing work with meaning than any generation in a century. Bravo.

Still, scratch the surface of the average corporation's sales department, and you'll still find the usual words: *cutthroat, ruthless, dog-eat-dog*. Amazon has contributed to this, too, because there aren't any salespeople at all, not even in their Amazon Go retail stores. The underlying assumption is that people are only driven by greed and that, unless you measure everything using cold figures, salespeople will slack off and lose motivation. In musical terms, we're back to Auto Tune and elevator music: industrial, inorganic, and cold. Nobody wants to listen to that.

No disrespect to Adobe, which is a very successful company, but when I went there in 2011 after twenty-two years at Apple, it was a shock to the system. They were a very traditional sales organization: numbers, metrics, numbers, metrics, and did I mention numbers? The attitude was, "It doesn't matter what the customer wants, this is the program we have, roll it out."

That doesn't work. I've been around the block a few times, and I can say with high confidence that all emotionally healthy people want to be creative, to find meaning in what they do, and to fill their days with passion and heart. That's why so many people dream about being musicians or writers even if they have no talent for either one: we all want to do what we love, what brings us joy. If we can make a living that way, that's heaven. The best salespeople I ever knew infused their work with that same passionate intensity—that music.

That's why, as *Fortune* says, millennials absolutely adore Apple.[6] To this day, the company radiates heart and soul. When I was there, the organization listened, absorbed what we said, had rhythm, and wanted us to be people first and salespeople second. In return, we were happy to jump through hoops and scale impossible cliffs. When you're just a number, you're cranking it out for a paycheck. When I was with Adobe, even though I did the second largest deal in their history (because I did it my way), it wasn't the same as Apple. It was soulless.

When selling is mechanical, it's like dropping to your knee and proposing to your girlfriend by saying, "My love, would you sign this paperwork so we can combine our assets and file a joint tax return?" Be still my heart. That's not just boring for the customers, it's boring for salespeople. Remember that when we enjoy what we're doing, we do a better job.

At Apple, we were always deeply human. To this day, when I see somebody having a great Apple experience, it warms my heart. I'll never forget a meeting in California. It was early in Steve's tenure, and we were still struggling to just stay alive. Jobs came out and sat on his stool, looked at us, and his first words were, "We're gonna make it. I will not let you down." That was stunning. That's why he was a leader. He took ownership of our fears and worries. We hadn't heard anything like that in years. What we'd heard was crap that disregarded the front line people carrying the Apple name, crap like, "These things sell themselves."

---

6   Reisinger, Don, "These Are the Brands Millennials Are Emotionally Attached To," *Fortune*, March 9, 2018, http://fortune.com/2018/03/09/millennials-apple-brand-intimacy, retrieved May 11, 2019

That was the first light of the real soul that would make Apple the greatest brand on the planet. Steve had a personal connection to our success. Sure, he was one of the founders, but I've worked for others in the startup world or at Adobe or other places for whom it was all economics and nothing else. From the beginning at Apple, we were never out to sell anything, naïve as that might sound. We were out to change the world. Internally, we used the phrase, "Computers are mental bicycles. They take you further and faster than if you don't have one." The focus of the organization was to improve people's lives through technology. That was the soul of the company.

That's hard, because most people aren't visionaries. Back then, selling tech was still about "speeds and feeds," so selling Apple's vision was an uphill struggle. We were able to do it because we approached our customers with heart and soul, not facts and figures. We were able to do it because the company cared about us, and we cared about the company. It wasn't just something we sold. We were all-in.

You Must Insert Yourself into the Customer

Years ago, during the era when a parade of ventriloquist dummies masquerading as CEOs marched through One Infinite Loop, my sales colleagues and I were at a meeting in New Orleans. The speaker was a newly minted Apple CEO—a German gentleman who lacked command of English idiom, and I know this because at one point he told us, "You must insert yourself into the customer."

I turned to the guy sitting next to me, who sold to the high school market, and said, "I think in your case, that would be a felony." Sometimes, when a line calls to you, you have to answer; am I right?

Kidding aside, what Dieter or Diesel, or whatever his name was, meant was valid even though what he said was more like a description of what happens in bad amateur porn. You do have to get inside the customer's head, and the way in is through the soul.

That's why the Apple Stores are so extraordinary. Come with me in your mind's eye, and let's walk into an Apple Store location:

> *You enter a clean space filled with light. Before you are tables lined with iPhones, iPads, MacBooks, Apple Watches, iMacs and more, ready for you to pick up and try out as much as you like. Toward the back is the Genius Bar, where you'll find people in jeans and T-shirts who know more about Apple products than you ever thought possible. Near the Genius Bar is a wall-sized video display and a sort of open-air classroom where kids and adults can take free courses. There are no strategically placed racks of product designed to tempt you. Store employees walk around helping customers, and as you walk in, one of them says, "Hey, how's it going? Help you find anything?" You say no, you're just looking right now. A nod, and she goes back to what she was doing. But when you finally do ask for assistance, whatever employee helps you is one hundred percent fully present—really listening and genuinely excited to help you find something great. You know you'll never find salespeople who follow you around the store or cashiers who say, "Thanks" robotically while not making eye contact. The Apple Store is an experience like no place else.*

Imagine if someone did that with the experience of buying a used car? Actually, Internet startups like Carvana have taken advantage of the fact that buying a used car represents the worst of old-school selling to create brands that free buyers from that horror. But the Apple Store is the most obvious proof of the secret ingredient behind Apple's success in sales and everywhere else: *love.* Account executives, engineers, designers—none of us could have done the extraordinary things we did or created extraordinary experiences for our customers if we hadn't loved what we were doing and the company behind us.

Under Steve, Apple got inside each of us and communicated a clear, powerful message: *Give us your best and we'll give you whatever you need to be your best.* The products were brilliant, but they only happened because of a family of soulful individuals who found themselves freed to express their passions, obsessions, and insane ideas in an environment where those ideas would not only be respected and heard but praised and encouraged. Steve unleashed the company's heart and turned us loose to be the best versions of ourselves.

The Apple of 1988, when I joined, had soul. It was all about change. The arc of that company took us from $100 million in sales all the way to being two weeks from extinction. But the disease that nearly killed us was cancer of the soul—the draining of our emotion and passion. It was the Mac clones and the beige boxes and the push to be just like everyone else. It was fear. Steve pushed out the fear and brought back the music. It was like we all remembered who we were again.

Again, that's the difference between leadership and management. When we were living in that soulless world of logging our sales calls, we were being managed. The culture was dry and empirical, and selling was the same. Keeping the trains running on time is important, but it never inspired anyone to do anything more than make their numbers.

Steve's return inspired us to care and take risks. Make no mistake, he was a lousy manager. He didn't give a damn about the day-to-day operations of the company, other than the free coffee in Café Mac. But over in sales, we became individuals again, not numbers with a quota. We stopped thinking, "Me and them," and started thinking, "Us."

When you're selling, that makes a world of difference. If you want to insert yourself into the customer (ahem), you have to care about what they care about. That's impossible when you're convinced your company doesn't care about you—when you feel like the only thing that matters is making your number. When that's the case, the customer becomes nothing more than a means to make that number. Why spend an extra minute learning about his dreams or fears when that's one less minute you have to get to your next sales call?

Remember, Apple's darkest days were defined by fear. Our leaders feared being different, feared innovation, feared IBM and Microsoft. They probably feared their own shadows. Sales at its worst is about fear too. You're indifferent to the person sitting across from you because your only goal is to close the deal. You're afraid that if you don't, you'll lose your job. When selling becomes soulless, customers sense it. They aren't stupid, and they despise being treated like vehicles for your commission. I learned this when that crazy, roller coaster joy came back to Cupertino:

Make the customer feel small, and he'll think small. Make him feel big, and he'll think big.

Yes, making your number is important, but great selling is about more. When everything about your culture says you're valuable for who you are, not just for what you can produce, you're free to be yourself in the sales environment. That's why Apple Store personnel are so relaxed and easygoing; they're not under pressure to sell because Apple's DNA is about soul, loving what you do, and creating wonder. The company knows today, just as we did back then, that if you bring those qualities into sales, sales resistance drops to nothing.

That's about soul. When you look into the audience at a soul concert, or when you look into the congregation at a church while the choir is singing a bring-the-house-down hymn (almost all soul has its roots in gospel), what do you see? People on their feet, arms in the air, eyes closed, singing along at the top of their lungs, lost in ecstasy. They feel ten feet tall. If you could evoke even a small fraction of that joy in your customers by caring about what they care about, do you think you could set a few sales records?

I'm not being an idealist. The goal is still to close deals. That's how you stay in business and pay your bills. At Apple, we made our numbers (and then some) while keeping a structure and culture within which everyone could express their individuality and creativity. Smart companies, sales VPs, and sales professionals get it: the best way to make your numbers is to quit selling facts and fear, and start selling with soul.

Stop trying so hard. It's jujitsu-selling—selling by *not* selling. Individual contributors will enjoy their work more, managers will get better results, companies will earn more revenue, and customers will feel respected and acknowledged.

An Annoying Musical Interlude

One of the more bizarre episodes in the history of popular music involved the Queen of Soul, the late Aretha Franklin. Or more accurately, it involved an Aretha impostor. In 1969, a remarkable young soul singer began performing around Florida, billing herself as Aretha Franklin. Only she wasn't Aretha; her name was Mary Jane Jones, a gifted young gospel singer from Virginia who had always dreamed about being like her idol, Ms. Franklin. A James Brown impersonator named Lavell Hardy had Jones travel to Florida and forced her to perform under threat of violence, telling promoters that she was the real deal. Apparently, Jones looked and sounded a lot like Aretha, but the hoax could only work for so long. A few weeks later, police arrested Hardy and Jones. The young singer became a media sensation, told her story, met Duke Ellington (who wrote six songs for her), and became a successful performer in her own right.

The lesson: Soul can't be faked. If it's not real, everyone will know it. Real soul will earn people's respect and admiration. Be who you are.

Pieces of Soul

You don't go into music to get paid. Believe me, I know. I was one of the lucky ones, because I made enough to pay my rent. But I had to work every gig and studio session I could book just so I could afford to eat. No, you play music because you can't *not* play it. It's in your gut. It's part of you and, without it, something inside you withers and dies.

I can recognize the same quality in great salespeople. They're not just making calls. There's a fire in their eyes to tell somebody about the product, service, or company that they represent. Put it this way: mediocre sales professionals answer calls, but great sales professionals answer a *calling*. Selling, persuading, taking people on a journey through a landscape that you love—it's like a drug. When you're on it, you're high.

After I left Apple, my wife always knew when I came back from a meeting that hadn't had that joyful, musical energy. She would say, "Oh, I guess it didn't go well."

I was always surprised, because I would try to be buoyant and cheerful, but she saw right through me. "How did you know?"

"Because when it doesn't go well, you come back exhausted, and I can see it in your face." That's the thing about soul. It takes everything you have. If you're selling from the heart and the audience is giving it right back, you're fired up. If the crowd doesn't care, it can drain you dry.

Soul is one of the most challenging pieces of the Apple sales formula to get right because it's ephemeral. You can't schedule it. You can't write it down. You have to feel it. However, because "making my numbers" means giving you something concrete that you can use, there are some core ideas that can help you develop soul in your organization or find it in yourself. I've taken the liberty of naming each one after a classic soul tune.

"Think," Aretha Franklin

The first component of selling with soul has to be knowing who you are, being who you are, and taking pride in your identity. As the saying goes: "if you don't love yourself, you can't love anybody else" (also used by RuPaul). If you know what your values are and what's important to you, you'll bring those into your relationships with your customers.

At Apple, we had an exceptional team of people who knew themselves and were proud of who they were, what they cared about, and what they stood for. I think the company attracted strong personalities, especially after Steve took the wheel again. That also meant a lot of people didn't stay because they couldn't adapt to a soul-centric culture, either in sales or any other department.

If you're a manager or executive, it's in your interest to create an environment that encourages your account executives to show up as who they really are, not as faceless drones. If they feel seen and respected, they'll enjoy their work more and get better results.

If you're an individual contributor, you can't control the larger culture of your organization, but you can control how you show up every day. Show up with your head high, leading with your values and, by all means, be real one hundred percent of the time. Never compromise on the ideals that make you love selling. When you're trying to connect with what's in your customer's heart, authenticity is everything. If a customer feels that you're being manipulative or cynical, they'll shut down, and it's game over.

If they believe you're being vulnerable, open, and real, you'll make the kind of connection that gets them dancing in the aisles and giving you referrals.

"(Sittin' On) The Dock of the Bay," Otis Redding

This famous, languorous song is about patience and peace when things look like they might not ever change. To sell with soul, you need the same thing. What makes soulless, facts-and-figures selling so tempting is that it yields quick results. You go into a meeting with one goal—get the signature—and if you walk out with the deal, you're happy. But that kind of selling can cost you in the long run.

When you're head-down for the fast close, you can miss bigger opportunities that might take longer to develop. Dr. Marjorie Hoy, a world-renowned entomologist at the Institute for Food and Agricultural Sciences at the University of Florida, won a competitive grant for about $50,000. She was already an Apple customer, but her need wasn't suitable for the Mac, so I told her she should buy another platform. Essentially, I left $50,000 on the table. Nine months later, she received another grant for six figures. She called me, and this time her need and the Mac were a perfect it. We closed the business. I'll trade six figures for five anytime.

For you individual contributors out there, this is where you have to teach your leaders about "the more lucrative opportunity." Today's quick dollars are not always the best way to further a relationship. Also, when you're all about the kill and not the person, customers can sense it. So while they might give you their business once, you've done nothing to build a long-term relationship. In fact, you've probably damaged your chances.

Selling like we did at Apple can take patience. Yes, sometimes you'll walk out with a huge deal after your first meeting. But if your objective is to share what you love and lead with your heart, the close could take longer. But it will almost always be bigger, more satisfying, and more sustainable. Sit in the morning sun, and wait a while.

"Ain't Too Proud to Beg," The Temptations

In general, salespeople are terrible about asking for help. The traditional view of selling is of sharks in suits who get crushed if they show an ounce of weakness—and admitting that you don't know something is weakness.

Balderdash. At Apple, we were never afraid to confess that we didn't know something or weren't sure of the best way to communicate with a particular customer. That's how we helped each other. Being willing to admit you don't have all the answers isn't a sign of weakness but of maturity and wisdom.

The word you're looking for is *humility*. Sales professionals aren't known for it; in fact, the stereotype is one of bluster and false bravado. But great sales pros are humble. They ask for help. They bury their egos so they can serve the customer. They put the company's and customer's mission before their own *com*mission. (How's that for nifty wordplay?)

Wait, didn't I just say that selling with soul means taking pride in who you are? Yes, but that doesn't preclude humility. You can be proud of what you stand for while being humble and grateful that you're allowed to serve others in such a terrific profession.

"I Feel Good," James Brown

Don't take James Brown as an example of personal behavior. The Godfather of Soul was a notoriously difficult man, accused by those who knew him of being violent, dishonest, and impossibly demanding. This classic song, however, says it all. Selling should bring you joy, like it did for us at Apple. Your company and culture should lift you up, not beat you down.

If you love your company and find what you're selling inspiring, let that show in your relationships with your customers. On the other hand, while there might be cases when you can find the joy of selling a product or brand without a soulful environment behind you, that's really hard to do. If your employer would rather have an army of sales-bots instead of individuals who think for themselves, all you can do is seek greener pastures.

Look for a "fit" that brings you happiness and joy and respects the individuality and emotion you bring to your work. I was lucky enough to have that, and you deserve the same.

A Few Words on...Groove

Soul music is practically synonymous with the idea of the "groove," that period (sometimes an entire song) when the rhythm and instrumental drive of a song perfectly match the emotional intensity of the vocals and the lyrics, making the song infectious and irresistible. If you want to hear a terrific example, listen to the classic "Use Me" by Bill Withers, with its propulsive drum and bass line. It's groovy. Now, what does that have to do with selling? Well, while you might attain perfection once in a while, you'll never stay there. You could be in flow with a customer, telling a story so good that it feels effortless, thinking, "I am *the man!*" But at your next call, you reach for that perfect groove and it's not there, and you panic. Don't panic. The perfect pitch or connection is elusive, but the important thing isn't that you always have it. It's that you're always chasing it. Keep finding new ways to show up as your best self. That's how you actually deliver your best results while never settling.

Should I Stay or Should I Go?

Regarding that idea of fit (a subject worth reading about on its own in magazines like *Inc.* and *Forbes*), I get this question pretty often when I talk about Apple: "When things got bad after Jobs was ousted, why did you stay?"

The answer is important because, as I hope is clear by now, soul is one of those qualities that a workplace either has or doesn't have. For the most part, you can't create it; it's a reflection of the leadership. Workplace culture flows downstream from the C-suite. If your leaders aren't really leaders or they don't care about bringing passion and inspiration to selling, infusing the organization with those traits will be an uphill slog. You might be able to find that passion for yourself, which I will get to.

After Steve was gone, Apple suffered under a series of managers pretending to be leaders. How do I know they weren't leaders? Because:

Leaders add soul to a company. Managers can't.

When an organization has soul, passion, and that drive to walk through fire for the common good, that becomes the motive force behind everything its people do. I know because that's how we were at Apple. We would have run through brick walls for Steve after he came back, but it wasn't him we were in love with; it was the atmosphere of self-actualization and possibility he created. Steve was confident and secure enough that he didn't need to be an object of worship. As long as we were helping bring his vision to life, he was happy. That's a genuine leader. Leaders don't need to be idolized. They can bring soul to a company because they aren't threatened by it.

On the other hand, the best a manager can do is not deplete the soul the company already has—keep things running smoothly and stay out of the way. That's the best-case scenario. The worst case is when you have what we had—insecure managers acting like leaders. Their egos can't tolerate not being the center of attention, and that turns qualities like passion and joy into threats. If your manager wants all activity to revolve around him, he'll be a soul killer.

Faced with that kind of management, why did I stay? For one thing, crisis became commonplace after a while. I went through a lot of layoffs, including one where I was literally the only higher education account executive left on the East Coast. The rule was, if HR called you before noon, you were gone. If they called you after noon, you stayed. They called me right at noon. They said, "Hey, guess what? It's all yours. There's nobody else left on the East Coast." I went from handling five or six major university systems to fifty.

But I had been through so many layoff calls that I didn't even care anymore. Lay me off, don't lay me off. I ended up staying and stayed all the way through the $750-a-share era. But while the financial reward was nice, I didn't need the income to feed my family. I stayed because I loved what I was doing, even though I hated the company Apple had become. I loved my customers. I loved talking with them. I loved taking them on an idea journey. That was great for me. That's what I enjoyed doing then, and I love doing it with donors today. I still love solving problems. Great salespeople are problem solvers.

But I also stayed because I always knew that the organization had the soul to stand up to the bad management we were living with. I believed that if we had the right leadership—real leadership, not the Confederacy of Dunces—Apple's people would shine. And I was right. Culture is the collective soul and spirit of the individuals that make up your organization. There's nothing else there. We were all in it to change the world, and that's why so many of us stayed. Others who were just in it for economics left and moved on.

The Road to the Stage—Manager

If you're a manager, accept it. Organizations need people who keep the trains running. There's only a problem when you pretend that you're all about soul, vision, and inspiration when that's not really your skill set. Our problem after Steve left in 1985 was that we had a series of managers who wanted to be leaders, and leading means defining the culture and the vision. But they weren't visionaries; they were meeting-holders and consensus-builders. I'll say it again: *Know who you are.*

Tell your team, "Look, I'm a manager. I'm not a leader. I expect you guys to make the breakthroughs. I'm gonna expect you guys to take us to the next level. I'm gonna sit back here and manage it. I'm gonna keep the accountants and lawyers at bay. I'm gonna ask you to get your reports in on time. And other than that, I'm not gonna bother you."

People will respect you much more if you're honest enough to recognize your role and be amazing at it rather than trying to play an instrument that you lack the ability to play.

The Road to the Stage—Individual Contributor

The person in the spotlight can drip with soul even if the ensemble doesn't have much. Aretha, Teddy Pendergrass...

they set the feel of the song and expected the band to follow. Soul is an elusive thing, but when you're in the field,
you're in the spotlight. It's your show. I don't care if your company discourages its account executives to do so much as
crack a smile when meeting with customers. Trust me, if you
get great results, they're not going to care if you take meetings wearing nothing but a tie and a smile (do not try this at
home).

Soul, passion, authenticity, inspiration—they work. I know.
They are the sales pro's secret sauce. I'm a strong believ-
er in the "It's better to ask for forgiveness than permission"
theory. If your culture has no soul, and you're not ready to
leave, be a one-person Soul Train. If you generate twice or
three times the sales of your colleagues, things will change.

How to Find the Soul in Your Selling

The night's getting late and the band's getting tired. It's getting to
be that time—time to move toward the end of this book (please
hold the applause). So let me succinctly hit on some of the other
keys to infusing your selling with soul.

TURN THINGS AWAY

If you want a great organization, only do what you care about.
Someone once asked Steve what his greatest accomplishment
was, and he replied that it was the things he'd said no to, because
that gave him more time to do the things he really cared about.
Soul is about being passionately in love with life as a sales professional, and if you want that life, why saddle yourself with anything
you're not crazy about?

Steve had a reputation as somebody who always hit it out of the
ballpark, but he was honest and self-aware enough to acknowledge that wasn't true. He was proud of saying no. At the risk of

throttling this metaphor, sometimes hitting it out of the ballpark means saying no to getting up to bat.

Aaaaand that metaphor's dead. Moving on.

TAKE PERSONALITY TESTS

I'm serious. Go out and take the Myers-Briggs Type Indicator personality test. If you're running a sales department, have all your field reps take it. (There are other tests, some valid and some bogus; do some research if Myers-Briggs isn't your cup of tea.) I've done a number of personality tests. I could tell you my personality and the results, but then you would stop reading.

The point is, because of the testing, I know my pluses and minuses. Know yourself, and stop being somebody you're not. That's what almost put Apple out of business. We were trying to be IBM or Microsoft or something, and we almost "me too'd" ourselves to death. Get data on who you are, and be that person. If you're not a fit where you work now, go somewhere that suits your type.

ATTEND TO YOUR WORK-LIFE BALANCE

There's a lot of debate over this topic in business schools and the business press. Some people insist that work-life balance is impossible if you want to get ahead and preach work-life *integration* instead—meaning, blending your working life with all the other facets, like fitness and child care.

Whatever. Call it what you will, the object is to have your week include time when you're not working and time that feeds your soul in a way that even the most satisfying work can't. For me, that might be music or other pastimes. I don't care if you take every Saturday and spend it working in your yard, take a long walk every day at lunch, or meditate in the middle of meetings. Give yourself the time and space to let your body and mind recover. That might mean pushing back against demands to work longer hours. Do it. No matter what they may think, your employer doesn't own you.

Do what you must to avoid the B-word: *burnout*. Burnout actually changes how your brain functions and how you respond to emotional distress. The only real fix is time away from work, time when you're in control and the only demands are those that serve you. Take the time.

SOUL IS THE GIFT YOU GIVE YOURSELF

Can you create soul for yourself even when you're in an organization that doesn't have it? If the leadership and the organization have no musicality at all, I would say no. Get out. It's a lost cause. But if there's still residue of music and soul and passion in the culture, as there was with Apple, then you can. I did. I found something to love in my work, and it sustained me until Steve came back and lit a fire under all of us.

This is about knowing yourself. I know my own personal musicality. I know what I can do well and what I can't. When somebody asks me to do what I do well, I knock it out of the park. A law of great selling is to know who you are, and if your situation doesn't fit who you are, it's okay to say it's not right. But if you can find joy and excitement in what you're doing, stay with it until things change. When I was playing live, there were plenty of times I walked out on that stage and nobody was clapping. Most people didn't even know we were there. But I played anyway, and I loved it. I was making music for *myself*. To hell with everybody else.

Michael's Excruciating Soul To-Do List:

- **Find your groove.** Figure out what you're best at in the wide world of selling, and build your field work around that. Maybe you craft killer slide presentations. Maybe you're a Tony Robbins-level speaker. Maybe you're brilliant at writing proposals. Make that the cornerstone of your selling.

- **Take more risks.** Account executives thrive on adrenaline; it's why we do what we do. If we wanted safety, we'd be behind a desk. But the more risks you take with your pitch, the kind of customers you call on, and the tools you use, the more exciting new ways to sell you'll discover. That will make your work more fun, and when you're enjoying yourself, you'll light up the sky. Yeah, you'll make some mistakes and get called on the carpet for some of them, but every musician's played a sour note or two. Go for it.

- **Get the band back together.** Human beings are social animals. Science shows that we're happier and healthier when we have a strong social circle. But sales can be a solitary profession—even a lonely one if you're on the road a lot. But if you're in a company, you have a circle of peers who know the challenges you face because they face them too. Whether you're an individual contributor or manager, do whatever you can to build camaraderie among your sales team. Find ways to spend time together, strategize together, even create your own internal "joint ventures" where you collaborate on new ideas. Being with peers is energizing and fun. Half the reason I went to rehearsal was the joy of hanging out with the guys.

- **Propose getting rid of activities that drain your soul.** When Apple was back under Steve's leadership, the first change that hit sales was the end of call reports. We didn't do call reports because our leaders knew we got things done and were moving the ball forward. They trusted us. That saved us work and made us feel great. An organization with soul doesn't need call reports because you're doing the right things for the right reason. If you're being asked to spend time on activities that make you feel negative about your work, propose changing or eliminating them. You might not get anywhere, but that will be one more signal that you need to consider leaving.

- **Use Glassdoor.** If your organization is a soul-free zone and you don't see it changing and are thinking of leaving, go to *Glassdoor.com* to read candid reviews of other companies that talk about culture, leadership, and more. It's a great way to get behind-the-scenes intel on potential employers.

CHAPTER 8
Orchestration

noun

| ȯr-kə-ˈstrā-shən |

1: the arrangement of a musical composition for performance by an orchestra

2: harmonious organization

Examples:

Queen, The Moody Blues, Yes, Electric Light Orchestra

Let's talk about harmony. As a drummer, I was never the person responsible for creating harmony in the studio or on stage. But I certainly appreciated it and saw what went into creating something like the gorgeous chords you might hear in a Crosby, Stills and Nash song like "Carry On"; or if you're looking for something more modern, a track by Pentatonix. Creating musical harmony requires musicians or singers who all know their parts, the humility to blend into the whole instead of trying to stand out, and above all, a leader who decides when the sound is right. Take away any of those and you have cacophony—cats fighting or fingernails scraping on a chalkboard.

All organizations need harmony, too, because the basic mission of any organization is for people to work together toward a com-

mon goal. In sales, it might not seem like harmony is very important because of that lone-wolf stereotype that so many people still
believe. But that's the old way. You're here to learn how Apple did
it, and a big part of our success was that sales functioned as one
part of a harmonious whole. Even if we were on the road selling
according to our own style and personality, we were all part of one
big Apple family: one message, one brand, one vision, and a sense
that we were all playing an important part in creating the music.

Throughout this book, I've talked about the difference between
leadership and management. Well, orchestrating beautiful harmony is definitely a leadership function. As always, it began with
the return of Steve. Prior to him coming back, we were just teams
in silos. We had a group that did this, a group that did that. But
when Steve took over, the organization was flattened. We weren't
drones anymore, sitting miles away from the gods in the C-suite.
Just like the piccolo player in an orchestra knows that without her
part, the piece won't be completely realized, we all had a renewed
sense that our contributions were important.

Management sat down with us in sales and said, "Tell me about
your day. What's missing?" We created our own internal CRM system, but not to collect customer data. Its purpose was to collect
information on how we were working with customers and analyze
what we could do better. We were Big Data before Big Data was
cool. It was the first time that the company focused on personal
learning. It was the birth of Apple University.

Apple University actually didn't launch until 2008, only two
years before I left. But its spirit was present long before that. The
name says everything—this wasn't training. This was about learning how to think in the Apple way while retaining your individuality. Management was focused on the individual. They weren't
trying to make us all the same, because we weren't. We learned to
think critically, ask hard questions, and see beyond what was in
front of our eyes. Because if we could do that, we could take our
customers on the journeys we wanted to take them on.

The idea for Apple University sprang from a few sources. First, Steve's deep affection for higher education. Second, our long, close partnership with colleges and universities. Remember, the only thing keeping the company alive in 1996 was the education market. The consumer was gone, and the business side was gone. So it was natural to name our training group Apple University, because we weren't really training people. We were teaching them how to harmonize with the organizations that they sell to.

Even the nomenclature was a huge nuance. Instead of thinking, "I'm going to training," you were thinking, "I'm going to Apple University." It's a big difference in perception, in pride. For years before we officially launched AU, I was learning how to harmonize with the presidents and provosts of these giant, complex organisms called universities. I had to know how to adapt to their way of thinking and behaving if I was going to sell to them.

All those under-twenty-five-year-olds who work in the Apple store? They've all gone to Apple University. They claim it on their résumés, because when they attend, they don't learn how to ring up a sale. I can teach a bonobo, or even a member of Congress, to ring up a sale. They learn how to think, move, and talk like an Apple employee. They learn the Dao of Steve, if you will. That's why they're all on the same page and why every Apple Store interaction is so pleasurable. Going to a university doesn't just teach you. It *changes who you are.*

When you want to create harmony, you don't assign people to training. You assign them to courses that promote higher-order thinking. That's what leaders do. When Steve took the wheel, management changed from running a team to orchestrating individuals into a harmonious whole. It made all the difference.

A Few Words on... Blend

When you're trying to create beautiful music, there's a constant tension between the different voices (meaning vocals or instrumental sounds) blending together and certain voices standing out from the overall sound. There are times during a song when a single voice should pop out of the mix: a guitar or sax solo, a drum fill, a soaring vocal lick. But most of the time, you want your guitars, drums, bass, keyboards, and horns balanced and harmonious, producing a single, tight sound that the ear hears as "the song." That's a great metaphor for blend within a sales organization too. If you're managing a sales team, you want people who aren't afraid to stand out and take a solo. They're the reps who ask tough questions, take risks, and try new strategies. But you also need them to blend into the larger whole—to represent the company brand and message faithfully when they're in the field. How do you get that blend? By respecting the artistry of each individual while giving them music (in the form of an inspiring brand, message, and mission) that they can fall in love with. It's not easy, but it's possible.

Recognizing Individuals

Great organizations have harmony among their departments, but they often don't know what making harmony entails. I've seen many companies whose leaders obviously thought that if they just gave their people the sheet music and ordered them to sing, they would harmonize. It never works that way, though.

A while back, I was at the Gaylord Texan Resort for a fundraising meeting, and a very large San Antonio-based computer concern called Sirius was there for a big annual shindig with about six hundred salespeople. Because I'm incurably nosy, I was looking over their posters and the information about their coaching sessions and breakouts...and it was *shockingly* clueless. I thought, "Oh my God, apparently marketing has written this and doesn't know anything about sales." It was all generic words and phrases, and when you write generically, you think generically. When you think generically, you get generic results.

That's an example of zero interdepartmental harmony. They had all their people here, but they had no leader driving a single vision. If Sirius had the leadership to get their voices working together toward some kind of harmony, I wonder how much further along they would be?

Apple under Steve was an authoritarian regime...to a point. The big picture was under his iron control. That's why in the 2015 movie *Steve Jobs*, they gave Michael Fassbender this line: "I play the orchestra."[7] That's exactly what Steve did. But while he set the tone, underneath that control was a lot of freedom for people to work together or do things their own way, just as each singer in a vocal ensemble will harmonize his or her own way. In other words:

True organizational harmony always teeters on the edge of breaking down into noise because it's the tension between individual ambition and leadership's control that makes it great.

Listen to some songs—"Ruby Tuesday" by The Rolling Stones or "Rio" by Duran Duran come to mind—and you can hear it. The harmony feels one wrong note from breaking down, and the tension is unbearable. Balancing a group of people who want to do things their own way—especially account executives, who are pretty independent—and the desire of leadership to keep everyone on brand and on message is like being Philippe Petit, who walked on a wire between the World Trade Center towers in 1974. The path before you is clear, but there's not much room for error, and if you fail it's a *long* fall.

Harmony is the composition of individual sounds into a seamless whole. One of the ways you do that in a sales organization is to recognize that each person is an individual contributor. When Steve came back, we literally reclaimed that title, *individual contributor*, and started using it again. Remember, words matter. That title recognizes that you are contributing to the whole. Pre-Steve,

---

7   Boyle, Danny, Casady, Guymon Colson, Christian, Gordon, Mark, Rudin, Scott. *Steve Jobs*, theatrical. Directed by Danny Boyle. Los Angeles: Universal Pictures, 2015.

you were this manager or that manager—account executive, account executive two, account executive three. It was that anonymous...or should I say *generic*?

Under Steve, the men and women who were physically seeing customers were recognized as individuals with unique talents. The master skill, of course, is blending individuals together into a cohesive unit, and Apple knew just how to do that. Each account executive was assigned a systems engineer to help with technical demonstrations in the field. I started as a systems engineer, so I knew how to work with them. But if you're a sales professional who's not used to working with techies, will you know how to harmonize with your engineer? Will you understand each other? Can you work together as a team, or is your relationship more like, "I'll just send in my systems engineer, and he'll fix what I sold you"? Are you partners or individuals?

With Apple, there was virtually none of that, and here's why. Pre-Steve, most of our account executives just did their thing without any coordination with their systems engineer. I didn't do that because I knew better, but plenty of guys just winged it. After the sale, you called your engineer and said, "Hey, what we sold them, was that right? If it was wrong, can you make it work?" Pardon me, but the time to check to see if you packed your parachute is not *after* you jump out of the plane.

Steve recognized everyone as a valuable individual contributor, including the field IT guys who were there to help sales. You knew you were valued because a) the company spent resources teaching you; b) leadership listened to your ideas; and c) they insisted that you toe the Apple line in delivering an exceptional experience. It wasn't enough to get the sale anymore; you also had to represent the company's creative soul. You had to harmonize. We felt proud of that, and we loved doing it.

We hired account executives for their individual skills, not because they could fill a role. I knew people who were hired with no sales experience but extensive customer service experience. We called them *development executives*. They were not responsible for a number but for taking existing relationships further. The customer knew this person wasn't responsible for a number, so they tended to open up. We actually hired PhDs for sales, because skill set analysis told us that, with the right individual contributors with distinct voices, we could better create a rich, harmonious whole.

Harmony Needs Orchestration

That's where we get into the heart of this chapter, orchestration. Orchestration is the planning and coordination of the elements of a situation to produce a desired effect. If that's not selling, I don't know what is. Orchestration is what takes your practiced technical skill and heart and turns them into a polished band.

But coordination and harmony don't just happen. Even if you're talking about a doo-wop quartet singing around a trashcan on a Philadelphia street corner, someone needs to set the tone and determine the sound. Orchestration requires a conductor or director to pull everything together into a harmonious whole.

Sometimes, that creates friction. Prior to Steve coming back, I never had a manager ride with me when I went on a sales call. After he came back, I couldn't get rid of them. Having what felt like a babysitter was irritating, but at first I didn't understand how they were helping me become better. The practice of having managers along for the ride helped me identify "hagelohs," those, er, unique mannerisms that I had and actions that I did without thinking about them but which really helped me sell. When the company started sharing "hagelohs" with account executives, that's when I started to think I should write a book. (The funny thing is, I had to write the book to figure out what I wanted to say.)

So this is Apple's fault. Not mine. Blame them.

What is a "hageloh?" It could be the way I would approach a certain sales situation or how I researched the situations I was going into. Know your audience, right? But my thinking was always musical. I might change the tempo of my own voice in a presentation. I might tailor my words (my lyrics) to the background of the person I was talking to. I became well-known for having great conversations with receptionists. Receptionists are important because they control the appointment calendar. I'll bet there are receptionists working for at least five major universities who still remember me from back in the day. They were usually grad students who loved anything that distracted them from the tedium of studying, and they liked that I made funny small talk with them.

But that small talk sometimes led to crumbs of information I needed to reach my goals. And guess what? My percentage of meetings with executives—the decision makers—was the highest in the company. I'm still the only rep to ever have a university president address Apple's worldwide sales team. Why? Because I could talk to her. I could get past the chief of staff because everyone knew and liked me. They gave me the benefit of the doubt.

Anyway, these managers riding with me were part of Apple's orchestration of internal harmony. They were coaching me, but they were also collecting knowledge and sharing it. I was learning from other field reps like they were learning from me. They were our conductors.

Play "Honky Tonk Women" Before You Play an Original Tune

But the critical piece of orchestration, and something that we had to learn at Apple over time, is that orchestration has a table of contents. It's essential to know what to do when. The order of your actions is everything. From a drumming point of view, I might want to start faster than where I want the tempo of a song to end up, but maybe the other players can't jump in that fast. So I'd start with a slower bass roll to get the tempo into their ears and establish the groove, then they'd come along with me to a faster beat. Some drummers start a tune with a cymbal crash or by playing the hi-hat to signal, "Here we go."

It's the same in a sales presentation. Some reps want to jump right into products and pricing, but that's treating the other person in the room like a means to your commission. There's a time to whip out the spec sheet and talk pricing, but how about starting with, "Carlos, last week was your anniversary, right? Congratulations! How many years?" That's the equivalent of a snare roll to kick off a tune: it gets things in motion at the start. I've lost count of how many meetings turned out positively for me because I was sensitive to the room and adjusted the order of what I did and said.

Orchestration puts the pieces in the right order, and that's much harder than it sounds. Apple had all the pieces. We had great products. We had decent marketing. But we had them in the wrong order before Steve returned. We were also leading with product features. We were presuming that putting the pieces in front of the audience was enough. It's not. If you put a boring gray box in front of a university president, he's going to stare at it like you just dropped a dead cat on his desk and say, "What the hell am I supposed to do with this?"

When you have orchestration, you sell with stagecraft and theatricality. You never assume that the value of what you're selling will be self-evident. You assume that people won't give a damn about what you're selling and that you have to *make* them give a damn. In a band, you don't just go on stage and start playing. You put on a show.

For example, building a set list is an art. If you're playing for a crowd that doesn't know your music, you don't start your show with a bunch of original songs, or you'll bore them to tears. You start with something they know, something they can dance to. Then, five songs into your set, you can play something that you wrote. Now they like you, and they'll listen.

An Annoying Musical Interlude

When it comes to pop and folk harmony, few bands measure up to Crosby, Stills & Nash. All wildly successful musicians with huge hits before they collaborated, David Crosby, Stephen Stills, and Graham Nash somehow managed to surpass their previous work with the incredible harmonies in songs like "Suite: Judy Blue Eyes" and "Wooden Ships." But their sound didn't come about as a result of long rehearsal. It happened spontaneously; instantly. The trio were hanging out at the L.A. home of Joni Mitchell, who had become Nash's girlfriend after dating Crosby (which must have made for interesting rehearsal banter). The three men met in Mitchell's living room, and Crosby asked Stills to play a song the two of them had been working on: "You Don't Have to Cry." Stills played it, and when Nash asked him to play it again, Nash added his higher, sweeter vocal to their two-part harmony, and the result was magical. The shimmering CSN sound was born, just like that.

The lesson: Orchestration and harmony never "just happen," but sometimes the pieces are in place for them to show themselves with the right push and direction. Keep your eyes, ears, and mind open for clues that suggest a person or group might harmonize well with you or your team, and be willing to try.

My Orchestration Mix Tape

We all have our humiliations from our youth, those secrets we would rather sleep on a bed of broken glass than reveal to anyone. But I'm about to reveal mine. Here goes:

Back when I was a youngster of eighteen or nineteen, I was really into disco.

I know. Can you still respect me? Wait, you didn't respect me anyway? Then we're good. Let's continue.

Back then, when disco was a thing, I was the host of a dance-oriented radio show called "The Music Show: Pro Disco." It got picked up as a Friday night filler program by a radio station, and while it never got syndicated, it hung on for a while, and I enjoyed it. Nobody older than me at the station cared about disco, and nobody younger understood it, so I was all alone at the right age for it. It sounds odd in today's world of on-demand streaming, but this was 1979 or 1980, and there were no shows in my area dedicated to party music. I was it.

At that time, we didn't have streaming or MP3s, and the iPod wasn't even a glint in Steve Jobs' eye. We had the Sony Walkman. In case you don't remember it, you put in a cassette tape, hit Play, put on your headphones, and voila! A personal soundtrack. It was also the era of the "mix tape," a cassette that you compiled of certain songs that fit the mood of a particular event, time, or even a person. You might create a birthday mixtape, a morning mixtape, and even a mixtape for your girlfriend. Well, my show was an on-air mix tape.

It was a class A station—100,000 watts of power—and we took calls. I built out a playlist using carts that I would plug in fast, which is how you can go from song to song in the twenty-two seconds of airtime you have while the commercial is playing. But my mix was special: fifty percent familiar songs and fifty percent rarities and unusual songs—what some people call "deep tracks." Everything would have the same feel depending on the time, the season, my mood, and so on. I could take the audience on a journey (a preamble to my days of taking customers on journeys), and I'd always get calls asking, "What was that song?" A lot of times, it would be the B-side of a single that was really good but never got any airplay. People liked my show because it was comfortable and friendly, and I took them places no other DJ would.

There's an organizational mix tape for orchestration too. (How's that for a segue?) It's not as varied as the mix tapes I used to make, but you can apply it in ways that get the best response from your audience. These are the tracks:

LEADERSHIP

Like I said, orchestration implies a director or conductor to shape the sound and ensure that everyone's playing their part. In a sales organization, that's your leader, and I choose that word deliberately. *Leaders* carry the vision and inspire their followers to blow past their limits; *managers* make sure everybody is punching their time cards, hard drives are backed up, and that documents are proofread. Both are needed, but only a leader can orchestrate a group of individuals into a harmonic ensemble.

The reason is simple: leaders are also artists. Managers are technicians. If you put a manager at the front of an orchestra or vocal group, every note might be pitch-perfect, but the piece won't have any swing or soul to it. It'll sound like it was played by a computer. A leader has a vision for the final sound of a piece of music, and he or she also has a vision for what a company should look like.

When you're trying to get a group of scattered account executives to collaborate as a unit, the only thing that will convince them is a vision of the future where things are better than they are today. At Apple, Steve's vision was of a company where we learned from each other and got better, and a brand that came with a story so compelling that our job was half-done before we ever stepped into the customer's office. We all sat up and listened to that vision, and when it came time to work as a unit, most of us played our parts. The ones who wouldn't play moved along.

A winning ensemble needs a leader at the head. If you don't have one, find one. If that's not an option, try handing the baton to someone who shows promise—maybe a new VP of sales with the charisma to get people on board with new ideas.

REPETITION

Acclaimed violinist and conductor Joshua Bell says, "Good conductors know when to let an orchestra lead itself. Ninety percent of what a conductor does comes in the rehearsal—the vision, the structure, the architecture."[8]

---

8   Mermelstein, David, "Bell Epoque," *The Wall Street Journal*, April 9, 2012, www.wsj.com/articles/SB10001424052702304023504577319492 102184730, retrieved April 24, 2019.

That's exactly right. Practice in your rehearsal space, repeating the same song fifty times until your ears are bleeding, is what makes you a tight, professional ensemble. Repeating collaborative sales tactics or ways of preparing sales materials and presentations is how you get good at using them. At Apple, we didn't just roll out of bed and become great at expressing Steve's vision in a day. It took practice.

Plan on a lot of hard, grueling work to get your sales staff and support people to play together nicely and to take the ensemble view of success—that is, when one person wins, everybody wins. That mentality can be a challenge in a sales organization, but if you drive it home consistently, it will catch on.

A GREAT MUSICAL SCORE

If you think of a musical score as the plan for an orchestra, or a chart as the plan for a jazz ensemble, then your plan for getting your people to work together in harmony is the musical score for your sales organization.

How will your account executives interface with their support personnel? How will you handle training? What is the company's vision and mission, and how will that be communicated to the sales team? How will they communicate it to their customers? How will you gather, log, and analyze customer data? How will your account executives share the good ideas, big and small, that they learn from customer interaction and turn them into organizational wisdom? Your plan should answer all these questions and more.

If you stretch the musical score analogy even further (and it's near the snapping point already, I assure you), you'll also realize that music occurs within a very strict set of rules for notation, meter, chord structure, and the like. Your plan should be as strict about rules that govern conduct and expectations for your salespeople. I'm not suggesting that you be dictatorial or try to control everything they do, because that will backfire. But creating clear guidelines for things like travel, reporting, and presentations means that your reps have fewer things to worry about, so they can spend more time and energy on building harmonious relationships within and outside the company.

A COMMITMENT TO THE AUDIENCE

One of the most important changes to Apple's sales culture after Steve came back was that we stopped being a data-first organization. We still had our numbers to make, of course, and we cared about our commissions. We also invested a lot of time in tracking our customer interactions and seeing how we could get better. But we stopped making the number of calls and the deals closed our top priority. Our mission became all about sparking wonder and excitement in the customer, because that was what Steve was all about. In other words, we stopped playing music for ourselves and started playing for the audience.

Making beautiful harmony and playing music in perfect coordination isn't possible when it's every man for himself. When players in a band or orchestra are preoccupied with being the star or standing out, they're serving their own egos. When salespeople focus on the numbers, they're about ego and greed. But when the customer becomes the reason you're onstage, you're happy to step back, blend in, and harmonize with your fellows because your number one goal is to make the customer happy.

That takes walking onto that stage already committed to serving the audience. In fact, it begins well before your reps hit the stage (or meeting room). You and your sales team have to create presentations and develop strategies from a customer-first point of view. How can you solve the customer's biggest problem or allay his greatest worry? How can you be the provider that creates delight where everyone else was just "Meh?" How can you be the one to tell him the true information he needs to hear while the other guys are blowing smoke up his backside?

When you're oriented on the audience, the only thing that matters is what makes gorgeous music that will get them dancing. Harmony becomes inevitable.

A Few Words on...Voice

I wasn't a singer, and believe me, you don't want to hear me sing. I was a drummer because I couldn't carry a tune if it had handles on it. But I know something about the power of voice, and in this context I'm not talking about a singer's voice. I'm talking about voice as the point of view and personality of your company. When you try to orchestrate the disparate parts of your salesforce into something harmonious, be sure you have a voice in mind. Your voice is the way your company and brand communicate with the world. It can be shrill, compassionate, funny, blunt—you name it. There are just two rules: your voice must be authentic, and it must be consistent. Create a voice that reflects the personality of your leaders, or you'll end up with something that feels fake and alienates customers. And don't change your voice once it's established without good reason, unless you want to disorient your market and sow doubt about your leadership. As for you and your sales force, you're like the lead singer for your company. You're the ones downstage, mic in hand, singing to the fans, feeling what they're feeling. So make sure you have a hand in crafting your voice.

The Architect of Nuance

After you-know-who, sales did something we had never done before: we did a company-wide assessment of where we were. Can you believe that even while we were in the throes of near-death, we didn't take the time to do that? It's true. But now, leadership looked over every detail in everyone's pipeline. We were assessing the orchestra. Did we have all the right players? Were they in the right place? Did they have what they needed to make beautiful music?

Eventually, when you've moved past the early stages, successful orchestration comes down to precision. In a complex piece of music, a single note or beat out of place, a single overlooked sharp or flat, can ruin the entire piece. That's why every detail matters—and why getting this right is such a challenge. It's why there are a lot of okay bands but very few truly great bands.

Let me put it this way: the most difficult thing I've ever had to play was the triangle, and I never want to try it again. I know that sounds ridiculous. Me, an experienced drummer who's played big live shows and played for some of the top acts in pop music, afraid of the piece of metal they use to call the ranch hands in for supper? It's true. It's an orchestration issue. I'm a good drummer, but the triangle is binary. There's just one tone, and you're either right or wrong. If you screw up, you can't cover it with a fill. There's tremendous pressure to get it right, and I can't stand it.

My theory is that this is why there are so few great triangle players (and few great tambourine players, too, but that's another chapter). The pressure is too great, because you're totally exposed. Once I was playing timpani in a classical concert, and I was pulled off it to fill in for someone on triangle. I love the big, rich sound of the timpani, and switching to the triangle was awful. I'm sweating now just thinking about it. The triangle is hard.

(Incidentally, if you think finding my address and mailing me a triangle as a joke would be funny, let me warn you. Do that and I'll find out where you live, drive up with my full drum kit, and play outside your bedroom window from midnight to 4:00 a.m. on a work day. Don't test me.)

At the highest levels, orchestration becomes about the small stuff. When you have the grand gestures down, nuance is the difference between good and art. Things don't come together the way they're supposed to unless someone is paying attention to every small detail, because at some level every small detail is important. A great conductor can go, "Third chair, second row, oboe—you're off the beat," because they can hear it. They can hear the percussionist sitting in the back and say, "Snare, you're driving us too fast here; slow it down and watch me." If you're leading a sales division, you're its architect of nuance. Your CEO should be the architect of nuance for your entire company.

Steve was ours. His perceptiveness and obsessive attention to detail gave us the extra ten percent we needed to get to "Think Different." If he'd been an orchestral conductor, he'd be the one saying, "Percussion, your timpani is out of tune by a quarter tone. Tune up." The timpani is a low-frequency sound, but it permeates through the entire orchestra. The same idea works for a company. Small details that few people notice make the difference between excellence and mediocrity. Great orchestration is about getting those details—that foundation—tuned just right.

For us, it was about knowing who we were, who we were going to talk to, and how we would communicate Steve's vision. We knew our customer and we knew ourselves. Those were the big musical lines. Once we had them, we layered on nuance—messaging, data mining, product applications, like layering shadings, dynamics, or lyric readings into a song when you've mastered the notes. The details make it sing.

Orchestration is hierarchical. You start with the basics, and as you ascend, you get more and more and more artistic. Finally, you get to that last ten percent where the small nuances knock the audience off its feet. Your mission—should you decide to accept it—is to know your music and your customer so well that you know exactly what nuances will blow them away.

How to Orchestrate and Get Your Harmony On

SHOOT THE MEETING

If you need to have a meeting to collaborate, you're in trouble. Some organizations go crazy with collaborative teams, but if you have to have a collaborative team meeting, you were never on the same page to begin with. At Apple, we had the kind of big meetings that Steve presided over, but we hated the kinds of meetings where everybody shows up groaning, you get the handout, somebody puts slides up, everybody says, "Great meeting," and then everyone goes back to what they were doing. Everyone hates those meetings. So we did what you may have only dreamed about.

We shot the meeting. Right in the head. Execution style.

Actually, Steve created a new meeting format. Your data and slides had to be sent to all the participants a day in advance. They had to be reviewed. When we got to the meeting, that's what we talked about. We didn't waste time. We debated the merit of everybody's ideas—"This is great, this is junk"—and we adjourned. That was it. Meetings became more interactive and a lot faster.

In a way, there were no more meetings. There were consultations and analysis. If the sales team did collaborate, everybody was in the same place when we got in the room, and we took apart whatever information we had. We were prepared, precise, and lethal. We didn't waste any time.

Meetings are like jam sessions with no goal and no timetable. If you're not calling them with a clear purpose and agenda, then you're just trying to feel and look busy. Try doing what we did. Take your meetings out back and shoot them.

KEEP IT SIMPLE

One of the things I hope will come through in this book is that very little that Apple did was rocket science. Our genius was keeping things simple, and that's hard to do. As I told you, when Steve took over, we went from forty-one products to four. That made everything simpler, including selling. But it's a lot of work to get to simple. Mark Twain said, "If I would have had more time, I would've written less."

Simplicity drove us to clarity. We cut our marketing department in half, not because we needed to lay people off, but because there were too many voices in the room. In the play and the movie version of *Amadeus*, Mozart talks about how opera is the only form of music where you can have eight different voices singing at the same time and still have a perfect harmony. Most of the time, too many voices lead to chaos. Lay the blame for that on a lack of orchestration. It's the job of the conductor or director to sort through the options, clear the field, and simplify the music for all the players.

Chaos is a failure of leadership. To make a successful new Apple, we had to pound the organization down and make it flatter. The way it was, we couldn't even see each other, much less hear the music other departments were playing and try to harmonize. We suffered from bureaucratic bloat, and so do most companies. Getting flat and lean makes room for the good stuff to come through clearly: messaging, great salespeople, great engineering. That's why one of the most important parts of great leadership is saying, "We don't need to do this."

I said earlier that one of Steve's greatest sources of pride was his ability to say no. That was a huge cultural change for us. We'd been playing to everyone, and when we started playing for select audiences, it was easier to play together. A great barbershop quartet only has four people, not fifty. Clear out what's not working.

BE COLLEGIAL

Harmony in sales and in business requires personal harmony. People have to like working together and respect one another. But that's tough when the atmosphere at a company is gruff and cold and all-business. Lighten up, people.

One of the changes I remember most vividly from Golden Age Apple was that when we got together to talk about sales, we were all required to talk about a win and a loss. That was a huge change from the past. At the original Apple, you couldn't talk about your losses; it was a fireable offense, if you can believe that. Nobody wanted to hear about our losses. All they wanted to do was glorify wins. It was like working for eight-year-olds who cried because they didn't get participation trophies.

Post-Steve, we were free to talk about losses. Everyone put their customer information in, and you broke down why it happened. It was painful, but it not only shed some light on where things went bad, it helped us commiserate and get closer as a team. We ended up winning more often because we were willing to talk about

our losses. Adobe was not that kind of culture. At Adobe, you began every Monday morning with a conference call. "Okay, give us
your wins, give us your pipeline numbers. Okay, how do you think
you're gonna end the quarter?" Nobody wanted to hear about
losses, just wins. That doesn't make the losses go away, but it does
make management feel good.

At Apple it was, "You have wins, you have losses. Okay, let's focus first on the losses. Was it a product issue? What it preparation?
Price? What could you have done differently?" The leaders had already looked at all the data because you had to submit it. When
you showed up, it wasn't a typical meeting. It was like an autopsy:
clean, clinical, quick. *Let's figure this out so you guys can get back
to doing that voodoo that you do so well.*

But there was a camaraderie and collegiality to it too. We saw
each other as colleagues, not rivals. You could say, "Guys, this is
what happened to me, can somebody help me through it?" And
another account executive who had been there before would say,
"Yeah, I read your report, this is what I think could have happened,
this is what I did in that situation last year..." It was great.

With Steve, Apple became more collegial and less business-
like, and that collegial environment led to greater harmony. That's
why this isn't about training, methodology, or systems. It's about
putting people in an environment where they feel not only comfortable collaborating but are rewarded for it, and letting them be
human beings.

When I was in the startup world in New York, I worked with all
these young Ivy League people at littleBits. After I'd been there for
a month, I held a "beer meeting" on a Friday at three o'clock. We
all sat down with an interesting selection of beers, and everyone
said, "Michael, we want Apple stories."

I said, "Before I tell Apple stories, let me ask you all a question.
Why are you all acting so corporate?" They were nonplussed. Finally, someone said, "Well, we're in business, and we just got $60
million in startup funds." I replied, "But you're all recently out of
school, so let's see some more collegial work, as opposed to build-

ing business departments. That was the secret to success at Apple. You want Apple stories? We didn't have structured departments. We were collegial. We let our hair down."

These gifted young entrepreneurs looked at me like the world had just opened up because they *wanted* to be more collegial, but they thought that being in business meant being *all* business. They had imposed that on themselves—a mistake that many organizations make. They were already burning the midnight oil, so they needed to let off steam. We were basically a big fraternity house of forty people, and I just freed them to relax and have a little fun.

What happened? We turned out better messaging, better product integration, better sales numbers, and better everything because we got out of that traditional mindset.

I'm not telling you to take a bunch of sixty-year-olds and try to get them to remember college life. It's a mindset, not *Animal House*. It's how you work with others. In a collegial environment, if you need to sit down with the Chief Marketing Officer over lunch, you do that. You drop the titles and status games and business faces and act like human beings. You connect, relate, and enjoy working together.

PAY ATTENTION

As a percussionist, harmony isn't a big thing. But it's a great thing for your ears, and it helps you play better. It sets the rhythm tonality, if you will. Human nature tells you when things are in harmony and when they're not.

Gerald Kidd, a professor of speech, language, and hearing sciences at Boston University, has studied something he calls the "cocktail party problem." It turns out that musicians are able to hear individual conversations in party environments much better than the average person, supposedly because they have become skilled at identifying and filtering out "white noise" that can mask language. I personally do that in large groups without intending to. I'm able to focus on what's being said even in a loud, crowded room, and that helps me make conversation.

The gist of this is that I've learned to focus my attention, and that's made me a better drummer and a better salesperson. Harmony takes not just listening, but *paying attention*. Attention is active. You're not just absorbing but analyzing and collecting information with the intention of acting on it. That's what leaders and conductors do. It's in their DNA.

The Road to the Stage—Manager

You're almost ready. You've got the mechanical pieces of live performance in place, and all that's left is putting it all together. Some of that will involve the things I've already talked about—killing off traditional meetings, fostering collaboration, and the rest. But don't overlook something you're uniquely equipped to do as a manager: be a great audience.

I ran into an attorney in Longview, Texas, who runs a large foundation. We got to talking about music, and he knew a lot. I said, "Do you play an instrument?" He said, "No. My talent is to be a great audience."

I thought that was terrific. Here's a guy who's been to law school and done all these other things, and he was comfortable in the chair he was sitting in. That is orchestration too: giving people permission to show you who they are.

Once, at littleBits, I was on the interview committee for a "full stack" engineer, someone proficient in all areas of software and website development. It's a very technical job. But I asked him about music, and he looked at me and said, "You don't want to know what coding languages I know?" I said, "No, I can get that from your résumé. I want to know about you." He went off about his desires, songs he liked; songs he didn't like. I hired him, and he's the best full stack developer we ever hired. He was technically competent, but we could test that. What we couldn't test was: did he fit in? Was he a salesman of ideas? Could he learn new skills? Once I knew who he was, I knew he could harmonize.

The Road to the Stage—Individual Contributor

In a cappella vocal groups, having a "good ear" is essential. You have to be able to hear harmonies taking shape and changing in real time and change your own pitch to keep building new chords. The same applies for guitarists, bassists, keyboard players...everyone. If you don't listen for the chord changes, the result is a discordant mess.

As an individual contributor, having a good ear for harmony means listening to the changes in things like culture, ideas, or even mood. Human beings are all about the delta—the change from one state to something else. That's when things become meaningful for us. That's why great stories are about conflict and resolution, rise and fall. The reason reality TV shows about celebrities getting addicted to drugs and then cleaning themselves up are interesting is because the change is what fascinates us. Apple probably would not be where it is today without the descent into beige-box Hell.

As you get closer to live performance, pay attention to the changes around you. Be ready to adjust your approach based on them. The more attentive you are, the more easily you'll adapt to any onstage situation.

Not Every Leader is an Orchestra Conductor

There's a difference between an orchestra conductor and a leader. Leaders say, "We're taking that hill no matter what." The conductor says, "If we do what we do well, we'll already be at the hill." All conductors are leaders, but not all leaders are orchestrators or conductors.

Great conductors, while they may not be able to play every instrument, have an appreciation for what each instrument brings to the organization. At Adobe, our CEO came from the very technical side. Like the silicon side. Discussions with him about customers and empathy—well, they were like talking with an engineer. Inflexible thinking. One license, one customer. He couldn't get out of his personal frame of reference to see the validity of how the ensemble approached things.

Today, he seems to have changed. He's morphed into a great leader, if your measure of that is a rock-solid stock that's been that way for years. But changing the world? That's not Adobe. A great conductor has a vision in his or her head of what the music should sound like in the end when everything comes together at a live performance. If you can only see part of that vision, you can lead, and you might be technically brilliant, but you won't make true harmony—that takes the ability to bring people together.

If you're a great player on your own, be a great player on your own. That's valuable. But don't try to be an orchestrator when you don't have that club in your bag. You'll end up being the one-man band at the carnival: the guy with the drum, the harmonica, and the cymbal. That's not music, people. It's noise.

Michael's Excruciating Orchestration To-Do List:

- **Take care of the gatekeepers.** I always take great care of receptionists and people like that. The same with hostesses at restaurants in New York. It's much easier to orchestrate outcomes when people are working with you, not against you.

- **Be a lubricant.** Get your mind out of the gutter. I mean, be the person who reduces friction in meetings, strategy sessions, on the road; whatever. That means being prepped, being efficient, having a Plan B, and being on time.

- **Ask the next question.** Sometimes, intel about a customer can be the key to making the sale. But it's tough to tease that information out if you don't ask for it. Ask what I call the "next question"—the logical follow-up that no one else will ask. These are often "why" questions that dig into motivations. Ask them even when it seems like everyone else wants to move on and then wait for the answer, even if it's "I don't know." Then figure out the facts.

- **Know the patterns of your ensemble.** If you're a manager (and even if you're not), the key to getting your people to sing in harmony can be knowing them as people and knowing when they're off their game. If you observe their patterns of behavior, you'll know when they're breaking the pattern, which can mean something's not right.

- **Bring a pencil.** Real-time changes to a musical score are common. Be ready to change the plan on a dime and adapt to the new music. The faster and more smoothly you do that, the better your results will be—as an individual and as a group.

CHAPTER 9

Magic

noun

| *'ma-jik* |

1. Something that seems to cast a spell

Examples:

Pink Floyd, Beyoncé, Michael Jackson, Prince

It was 1979, at the Palladium in Miami, Florida, and there was magic in the air. The audience could feel it. I was there, and I was anticipating…something. No one knew it, but that night was the official coming-out party for rap. The Sugarhill Gang came out and played "Rapper's Delight," and music would never be the same. Magic is hard to predict, but you know it when you hear and feel it—or when it's over and you miss it. Try it. Listen to "Rapper's Delight" with open ears and an open heart. It's magic. By the bye, it was preserved in the National Recording Registry by the Library of Congress in 2011. Take that, Taylor Swift.

If you've ever attended a concert like that one in Miami—or for that matter, a film, play, poetry reading, or other event—where what you experienced left you feeling transported and enchanted, you know what magic is. As a musician, when you're playing a live show and everything comes together in the moment, and you can't believe what you're hearing, and you're filling with joy and gratitude at being able to do this...that's magic. It's fleeting, and it's perfect; and it's what you're ultimately striving for, even in sales.

The irony is that nobody really associates magic with selling. Great product engineering, sure. Seamless user experiences, yeah. But not sales. Selling is the brute force part of business in people's minds—the necessary evil of capitalism. If we bring magic to the table, it's black magic, mind control; tricking people to sign on the dotted line. That's the popular conception.

Well, that might be the stereotype, but that's not how it was at Apple. In a very real sense, we in sales were the best magician's assistants Steve Jobs ever had. We were the ones pulling rabbits out of hats in the field and demonstrating the incredible new products the designers and engineers were dreaming up back in Cupertino. They got to sit in the office, but we were out on stage, weaving a story, telling a tale, and enchanting customers with what was possible. If that's not magic, I don't know what is.

We're past the practical parts of getting ready for a live musical performance and even past the "feel" pieces, like soul and harmony. Magic is the final goal. It's also the most ephemeral. You can't always make it happen. Sometimes your spells fail. In fact, they fail most of the time. What made Apple so incredible from about 2001 to 2010 was that our magic almost always worked. The iPod, iTunes, iPhone, iPad...has any other company ever had an unbroken series of blockbusters like that? That's why I like to say that Apple was Camelot, and if that's true, Steve was Merlin. That kind of magic is heartbreakingly fleeting; that's what makes it so special.

So your goal is to make magic for your customers, but magic is so tough to pin down that you might never manage it, right? Yeah, that's about the size of it. But it's the effort that matters. Casting the spell at all is what makes you great. So let's talk about magic.

What is Magic?

There's something that swells up in your heart when you see magic. It's transcendent. And it's elusive. Of the twenty-two Apple sales conferences I attended—global sales offerings and local stuff—there were very few times that the presenter was able to take us to another place. But Steve had that aura. Like in a magic show, everything was precisely put together. When all the elements blend—a perfect presentation, tempo of the words, the choice colors—you step over into this ephemeral feeling of wonder. You surrender to the performance, and you're happy to let the presenter take you wherever he wants to. It's this glorious sense of abdication.

I've attended and experienced just a few performances like that in my life, but I remember them all. What I've learned is that the really interesting thing about magic is how much goes into it that you don't see. I've talked about Steve's obsessive attention to detail when it came to presentations, but the reason he was so maniacal about the tiny things was that he knew what great musical performers and stage actors, not to mention magicians, know: it only takes one tiny failure to burst the bubble and break the spell.

Apple's neurotic engineering and software design, the attention we paid to the unboxing of our products, the painstaking focus on every facet of the customer experience at the Apple Store—those are acknowledgements of the fragility of magic and our responsibility to the Cult of Mac. Once you create the highest expectations of enchantment, you stop at nothing to meet them. That's why the most important person in a live performance to me (and I've done quite a few) is the audio engineer. Without that perfect mix, it doesn't matter how great the band is playing: the magic spell is broken.

Here's a great example. If you're old enough, you might remember when illusionist David Copperfield made the Statue of Liberty disappear on live television back in 1983. He assembled a group of spectators on Liberty Island, erected tall towers to cover the statue with a screen, and when the moment came—voila! The statue had vanished. America was astounded.

It took more than thirty years for the secret of the trick to finally be revealed. It turns out that Copperfield had built a massive rotating platform to hold the spectators and TV cameras, and when he was ready to make the statue vanish, he turned the platform so gradually that the people sitting on it didn't notice. At the same time, the lights went out, and the helicopters covering the illusion slowly flew in line with the platform's rotation. Since they were unable to see the statue because of the darkness and the towers that blocked their view, and couldn't detect the platform's turn, when the lights came up and the screen dropped, it appeared the statue was really gone. When I talk about preparation and attention to detail, that's what I mean.

For Apple, magic was the culmination of everyone's work. Even behind the scenes, nobody stopped working to create that mystique. For example, every time I saw Steve, he was wearing the same turtleneck. He never dropped character; that was part of his mystique. We had another CEO who didn't have it. Instead, he wanted to be everyone's best buddy, always slapping us on the back. There were plenty of sycophants who sucked up to him, but ultimately he took his own magic away and lost his power to dazzle and lead.

Part of being a magician is being larger than life. Neil Peart of Rush, who many people consider the greatest rock drummer, has that quality. I would never presume to walk up to him and ask how he plays the kick drum on the solo in "YYZ." That would be crazy. I'm a bit-player in the world of drumming; he's a wizard.

Someone like Gene Simmons of Kiss had schtick, but that's not the same thing. Pre-Steve, Apple was suffering from schtick overload. People would do corny leadership things instead of leading. They didn't respect something that Steve had tremendous respect for: the importance of wonder.

People don't just let themselves be fooled. They *want* to be fooled. They want to believe in the impossible. We never lost sight of that. Even from the Apple II days, the theme of the company was, "Never show what's underneath." We knew nobody cared about the inner workings of the computer, just like nobody today carrying a MacBook Pro or iPhone through an airport cares about the guts of the processor or the haptics. They care about what they can do.

That's the magic, and seeing how the trick works destroys the magic. You can track Apple's decline pre-Steve experience to when we started handing out spec sheets in sales. When we showed everyone how the trick worked, they said, "Oh, these work just like those Windows boxes, and they cost twenty-five percent more." As soon as Steve came back, the spec sheets were gone. The magic came back, and we were able to take customers on that journey again.

A Few Words on...Nuance

Nuance is the small stuff that everyone tells you not to sweat. Sweat it. That's what made Apple great. In a way, we weren't a tech company; we were a nuance company. Nuance refers to all the subtle details of a product, service, or performance that, when you add them up, are the difference between an okay experience and a mind-blowing experience that makes you a rabid fan for life. At a fine restaurant, that might mean the finish of the silverware and the typeface on the menus. With Apple, it meant everything from the startup chime of the iMac to the texture of our product boxes and the bags you take away from the Apple store. What makes nuance powerful is that it gets under your skin without you noticing. Small, wonderful details work their magic subliminally until before long, you realize you're hooked; and you don't mind at all. In musical performance, nuance is about tiny refinements in dynamics, meter, emphasis, diction, and even stage lighting. In sales, it can be about the paper you use to print materials, the words you choose, or even your cologne. The point is, the small things matter, and they add up. Never assume any detail is too small to obsess over. You never know what will produce magic for a particular customer.

Creating Magicians

But there's a deeper state of magic than simply enchanting some-one, and that's what I want to talk to you about. That's what really made Apple a world-class brand and sales machine. What separates the great spell-casters in any field from the run-of-the-mill guys sawing their assistants in half is not that they enchant and wow the audience. It's that their magic is *participatory* and *shared.* They don't just work magic; they give the members of the audience the power to work magic too.

While writing all this, I checked into a hotel and noticed a man checking in before me had a massive, almost coffin-looking piece of luggage. On it was written "Stryker," a brand of robotic surgical technology. I talked to him (because I talk to everyone; that's my superpower), and he represents tools that are life-changing to sur-geons. But they're also magical. Surgeons use Stryker robotics to heal and save lives, but what makes them magical is that they turn their users loose to create that magic in their own way. There's no predetermined outcome.

Real magic is collaborative. It happens when you, as a company or an account executive, deliver something that lets your customer be a sorcerer too. I've heard the iPhone called a "magic wand" be-fore, but it's really Steve's idea of the app store and the app ecosys-tem that was pure genius. The device, plus the software, turned the entire world into magicians! The idea that I can pull out my phone and with the tap of a virtual button send someone money, order food delivered to my door, and then summon a car to take me to the airport is incredible. That's being able to wave your wand and change the world.

Apple didn't hoard that magical power for themselves. They gave it to everyone. That's what a lot of other companies miss. They miss customer engagement. I never sold a thing in my life. I wove a spell. I took people on journeys, and my products were tools that could take my customer further along on the journey *on their own terms.* That's the key. In sales, whether it's one-to-one selling or selling a global brand, when your products empower the customer to blow past their own expectations of what's possible, that's money. It's your job to help them see their potential, get them the magic wand and spell book, teach them what they need to know, and then get the hell out of the way.

Many times I came back six or eight months after a sale to follow up, and people were so far ahead of where I'd thought they'd be that they had become the magician. They were happy to show me what they could do in a presentation or voice editing. Today, with artificial intelligence—machine learning is really the proper term for it—you can unburden yourself even more of drudgery so you can create magic. What is saying, "Alexa, turn the thermostat to sixty-eight and play *Pray for the Wicked* by Panic! At the Disco on the audio system," and having your house obey you, if not magic?

That's how we operated in sales at Apple. First we gave 'em hope and then we gave 'em a tool and then we gave 'em an ever-expanding set of tools because of the App Store. We unleashed other magicians. It was an extraordinary leap in business thinking. We're not just going to sell you a product, we're going to collaborate with you (or at least make you feel like you're collaborating with us) to unleash your creativity. Most companies couldn't care less about unleashing the customer's creativity as long as they close deals.

But the secret to that magical collaboration and the everlasting loyalty that comes with it isn't really in the products you bring to a meeting, or even the products your designers and engineers are coming up with in the shop. It's in why you go to the trouble in the first place. One of the things that always struck me about Apple products is how much attention is paid to tiny details and subtle functionality. You can go three or four layers deep in the functionality of your iPhone and find small tricks that are just delightful. None of that occurred by accident. Phones don't evolve. Someone created that functionality, and while you might think that was about anticipating user needs, there's more to it.

At Apple, our ethos was less about anticipation and more about guiding. It was, "See, here's how you can use this in a way that no one has ever thought of before, although it's really kind of a no-brainer when you step back and look at it." The idea of the iPhone user interface was to unlock the huge potential beyond the green "Send" button and red "End" button. When AT&T became the first carrier to take the iPhone, their then-head of technology sent Steve a one hundred-page document about integrating software into the handset. Steve just sent it back with "WTF" handwritten on it.

Apple's view was never, "Here are our tools and here's how they're gonna work." It was "Why don't you go here? Why don't you browse the web on your phone with a browser? What could you do if you did that?" That didn't work because the products were great. The products were great because behind all those nuances and cool hidden features were engineers and designers and salespeople who were having fun—who were as excited by the tiny details as kids on Christmas morning. You can almost sense the delight and the excitement behind every one of Apple's products, just like you can sense the joy in a great musician who's in the zone onstage. He's loving playing for the audience, but he's also loving playing for himself, too, and inviting the audience to share his joy and wonder is what brings them along for the ride.

Selling Magic

Everything I've shared with you to this point has been about getting you to sell with that same spirit. I approached selling with a theme of, "I want you to enjoy what I'm bringing you," not "Let's close a transaction." Plenty of times, I said no to a customer because they weren't feeling the magic, and that's crazy for someone who's responsible for a number. But somehow, I managed to get to $987,386,417.17 in revenue, gifts, and partnerships anyway (the creative in me rounds up the seventeen cents to $987,386,418, but who's counting?).

There were a lot of reasons for that—I knew the products, I prepared exhaustively, I cared about the customer—but one of the big ones was that I maintained a *presence*. All great magicians have a stage presence, a persona. Mine was being the guy who would make you laugh but tell it straight. I would steer you away from a solution that wasn't a fit, even though it cost me money in the long run.

I had one vice president of finance for a large, private Catholic institution in Florida. His assistant told me once, "He's been called on by hundreds of salespeople, but Michael, he actually wants to see you." There was something about me that got past his defenses, and I know it wasn't my good looks. I maintained a presence, and I think great selling does that. Apple's salesforce was always great at projecting a presence.

What do I mean? Well, presence is the feeling that you own the room, that everyone else is holding their breath and waiting on you to initiate the action. If you've ever seen a charismatic singer come out on the stage and a hush instantly falls over the crowd, you've seen presence. Now, that's not me. I was a drummer. I told people that my job was to sit in the back and look at assholes all day. But in a sales situation, I knew how to show up with presence. You take control of the encounter; you set the tone. You kick off with something fascinating, like the way a new product can change a customer's life, or a secret nobody else knows.

Ever see a great band like U2 make its entrance by just walking on stage and farting around for twenty minutes? No, because that's boring. Bono swaggers out and howls while The Edge rips into a solo on a song like "Vertigo." You do that in music and in sales. You grab the audience, make your presence known, and captivate them. Remember, you'll never bore someone into buying from you.

Doing that well takes an insane amount of work. Remember, way back in the chapter on Rehearsal (Chapter One), I talked about the amount of work it takes to make something look effortless? That's true times one hundred for magic. If you heard interviews with the late, great Ricky Jay, perhaps the greatest master of close-up magic in history, you'd find out that he had been working to perfect some of his tricks since the age of four. Incredible amounts of work and practice go into making what looks like a simple trick seem magical.

I remember hearing an interview with Teller, the non-speaking half of Penn & Teller, in which he talked about working to refine a trick where a red ball floats and moves around on stage like a pet dog. It was a favorite old-school trick of Teller's, but he says that it took him *seven years* of work and polishing to get it ready to be performed live. An incredible amount of literal sweat went into perfecting the incredible complexity that made it look simple, believable, and magical to an audience.

Some of the other critical pieces in casting a spell over your customer:

BREAKING THE FOURTH WALL

The fourth wall is that invisible barrier between the real world—the world of the audience—and the action on stage. Different art forms have stronger or weaker fourth walls. In classical music, the fourth wall is like a fortress; you'll never see the conductor or musicians even acknowledge the audience until an entire piece is finished. In theater, some plays break the fourth wall and have the actors address the audience, but many don't. Movies are the same way. For every *Deadpool* or *Ferris Bueller's Day Off,* which ignores the fourth wall completely and plays to the audience, there are hundreds of other films that treat the audience as invisible spectators.

But in live music, there is no fourth wall. The musicians play to the audience and draw energy from them. In some concert venues, the lead singer goes right into the crowd. Imagine Dragons lead singer Dan Reynolds is notorious for walking through an entire arena for twenty minutes, high-fiving and hugging his fans and posing for selfies. That's a level of intentional connection with the audience that you only see in music.

At Apple, we shattered the fourth wall. Because we loved the products ourselves and knew all the amazing stuff you could do with them, we could convey our enthusiasm to the customer in a raw, sincere way that they loved. That creates joy and connection. The products themselves did the same thing because we were so open about this "We want to collaborate with our customers to make your lives better" idea. Apple products were passion and engagement that you could touch.

LEAVE THEM WANTING MORE

Some of the best presentations I've ever done, where I had people stand up and clap at the end, have been the shortest. I left customers wanting more instead of overselling and pushing. Good sales professionals know that the real selling goes on in the minds of your prospect after you've made your pitch, and sometimes the best thing you can do is sing your song, take your bow, and make your exit, stage right.

I judge a presentation by how many questions I get when it's over. The more questions, the better I did, because questions tell me that what I said has people thinking. If I end and say, "Any questions?" and no one raises their hand, that's a failure. I've either put them to sleep, or I confused them by not meeting their expectations. They came for a blues concert, and I played disco.

GENEROSITY

Another piece of magic that ties in with music and live performance here is the contagious joy and delight you feel as a performer. When you're watching a live musical show, unlike a play, the performance isn't scripted. Sure, with classical music the artists are rigorously following a score, but in music, the artist is creating something new in the moment. When you're watching someone who is lost in that moment, overcome with joy, and having a great time playing for you, you can't help but get lost in that feeling too.

A real-life business example of that is John Legere, the CEO of T-Mobile. Now,

T-Mobile is effectively Deutsche Telekom, a German company, and Germans are not known to be the most gregarious people on earth. There've been entire marketing campaigns around how stiff and unfunny Germans are. But I went to see him give a talk, and the crux of his message was, "We're here to delight our customers." That's pretty radical for a telecommunications company. Most of them will settle for not infuriating their customers, and others in the space, like Comcast, seem to exist for the sole purpose of pissing their customers off.

But what really struck me was that for Legere, these weren't just words. He put the idea of customer delight into play at his company. One of their call centers is in Tampa, Florida, and I lived nearby at the time, so I visited and asked some questions. Turns out their plan was to give their telephone reps the authority to fix the situation, no matter what it was, up to a certain dollar point. So if a T-Mobile customer called with an issue, they weren't transferred around or handed to five other people like a bong at a college party. The person who answered the call was empowered to help them on the spot.

The result was a call center filled with front-liners who had the power to create delight and who liked doing their jobs because they were actually helping people. That's a big reason T-Mobile's customer satisfaction scores are off the charts. In fact, if I'm not mistaken, their reps still answer service calls by saying, "I can fix your problem."

That makes a much better impression than a recorded message saying, "Feel free to access all these services on our website at www.pleasedontcallusbecauseyourewasting ourtime.com." John wasn't on the front line, but he knew how to create magic by giving his troops the power to make some decisions. He wasn't your everyday CEO. He knew that treating customers like nuisances is the opposite of magic.

> ## An Annoying Musical Interlude
>
> Plenty of musical acts have been so popular that they drove their fans into a frenzy when they walked onstage. At the height of the Beatles' popularity, their female fans would scream so loudly that the band couldn't hear themselves play. They would throw their underwear on stage (I was never sure what that was supposed to accomplish; at least a hotel room key has a use), and after it got out that George Harrison loved jelly beans, fans would pelt the stage with them. But no one had the overpowering stage presence of the King of Pop: Michael Jackson. When he walked onstage at the beginning of his "Dangerous" tour in 1992, he hadn't even starting singing before people could be seen sobbing and fainting all over the arena. One venue reported that as many as five thousand concertgoers became hysterical or fainted during one of his shows. At another big show in England, so many fans rushed the stage that more than 1,500 were crushed and had to be treated for injuries. Hmm, at my shows, the only rush was to see who could be the first person to get out into the parking lot...
>
> **The lesson:** You don't always know what effect you're having on your audience. Sometimes, your impact won't show itself until later. Don't worry about ovations, and work your magic. The rest will take care of itself.

Showmanship and Mystery

The best salespeople, like the greatest magicians and musicians, have mastered the art of stagecraft and showmanship. They know how to hold something back and create a sense of mystery and drama. Steve was brilliant at both, and not just because he was obsessed with operational security around Apple's new products. He also did that with his personal image. Brilliant as he was, he could be off-putting, weird, and downright rude.

Once I had a customer in California walk up to him to shake his hand, and Steve just got up and walked away. We were working to close a $69 million deal with a school district in South Florida, and the superintendent wanted to get a picture with Steve, who was sitting at a small round table in Café Mac. The customer walked up, introduced himself, and said, "Hey, we just did a $69 million deal with you." Steve looked at him like a bug on a windshield, got up without a word, and walked away.

There's showmanship in holding back or being a little bit un-knowable. I've coached a lot of younger folks in the startup world, and they're all very quick to give you everything. One of the things I teach them is that stories play out over time, and selling is a story. If you want to have your customer in the palm of your hand, hang-ing on every word, make him wait for the good stuff. Be elusive.

When you get to black belt level with this stuff, you'll be man-aging your "aura." God knows Steve had an aura, and I think it was something he was very aware of and worked consciously to culti-vate. He could be the most confounding person imaginable, im-possible to figure out. On one hand, he was insane about details, but then he would show up for private meetings with the sales teams and stroll onstage with no production whatsoever. He was simple and complex at the same time.

At the Santa Clara Marriott, the last time I saw him before he passed away, the guy just rolled up in his Mercedes. There were two traffic cones marking his parking spot. He came through one, two, three doors onto the stage and started his talk. No introduc-tion, no fanfare. But for all that simplicity, he wasn't familiar or easy to talk to. He was aloof and distant. That was part of the aura.

Many great people, it seems, are difficult to know. They're awk-ward, obstinate, hot-tempered, or neurotic. That's part of the pack-age. They don't play by the rules—often, they don't even know the rules exist. You always knew when Steve was at Infinite Loop because his car was parked in a handicapped spot. It was closer to the door. You'd see a Mercedes with no license plate in the handicapped spot, and you knew he was there. But for all that, he didn't have a special entrance. I've seen CEOs who had their own private entrances to their buildings, like they're trying to avoid mingling with the hoi polloi. They have an entourage.

Steve didn't have an entourage or private entrance. He had this contradictory, strange, maddening persona that he never dropped. Maybe it was one hundred percent authentic, and maybe he was just very good at maintaining the façade. Probably a little of both. But he never let it drop. He knew that the moment you allow a crack in the aura, you break the spell.

In selling, it's to your advantage to cultivate an aura. It should be built on who you really are; you can't manufacture something that will resonate with people. Steve wasn't an easy man to know, and he didn't shy away from that. He didn't create a likable persona; he created a real one. Be who you are, only dialed to eleven. Add some showmanship: holding a little something back, building the drama, telling a great story. That's how you own the room before you're even *in* the room.

A Few Words on...
Knowing What the Audience Wants

The music world is full of manufactured acts, boy bands, and singers groomed and packaged and produced to appeal to a certain demographic. The Monkees were probably the first, but there have been many others. Sometimes they have hits, but nobody respects them, and they rarely last for long. What sets them apart is that they pander. Their managers and producers try to figure out what their fans will like, and then they record it. That's a recipe for mediocrity, and mediocrity is quickly forgotten. In sales, if you market research everything and think you know what customers want, you can focus group the magic right out of your business. I've been in front of customers for years, and they don't know what they want. It's your job to *know* what they need and *tell* them what they want. You guide them toward what you're sure will be thrilling and difference-making for them, and let your passion do the selling. If you're wrong, let them tell you. But if you're right, they'll regard you as having a preternatural gift for understanding their needs before they do. That's when you're working magic.

The Magician and the Technician

I've been heaping praise on the spellbinders and the audio engineers in this chapter, and there's a good reason for that: you need them both to put on a captivating show. Artists and technicians both play a role in creating something transporting; I can't tell you how many live shows I played that were less than they could have been because an engineer created a muddy mix, a lighting tech couldn't get the spotlights timed right, or the HVAC system was set on either Sauna or Meat Locker.

Magicians have to be technicians, but they can't do it by themselves. That's why Apple was so smart to send its account executives into the field with systems engineers like me when I first came on board. They were the magician, weaving a verbal spell, and I was the technician, showing off the bells and whistles. That's why Steve and Tim Cook were such a perfect team. Steve was an absentminded, right-brained genius while Tim fixated on details, timing, reporting, and all the left-brained tedium. Tim's attention to making sure schedules were met, designs were approved, and vendors were paid made Steve's sorcery possible. Without both, Apple's Golden Age would not have been possible.

The funny thing is that once I went into sales, my technician side went into storage. I rarely knew model numbers—no, that's not true, I didn't *care* about model numbers. Most of our models started with the letter M. I knew that. I didn't need to know models, speeds, or feeds. My job was to take the client on a journey and enchant them with possibilities. That was the musician in me. I know reps today who can cite product lines, model numbers, and prices in seconds. They're not magicians.

Magicians have respect for wonder. Go ahead and sell features and benefits if you want to, but you'll be just another salesperson, forgettable and interchangeable. Magic means selling a picture of what can be, of how your product or service can change the customer's business or his life for the better. That's subtle and crafty work, like making a ball float or a statue disappear. It means thinking of yourself as an artist, which should be easy, because you are.

How to Cast Your Spell

PLEASE YOURSELF FIRST

Magic is about pleasing yourself. However you approach your sales, it's about giving yourself joy. Bring the same energy as a director making his first film or a musician recording her first album: giddy, reckless, instinctive, and real. Whether you're developing a pitch or a presentation and you do it for yourself first, your joy becomes palpable. If you're pandering, customers will always know and resent it.

Apple took a huge risk when Steve came back—or maybe it wasn't a risk at all because he really did see what nobody else could—and we said of the iPod, "Here it is. We created this because we think it's cool. We didn't talk to focus groups or do market research. But we think it's awesome, and if you don't like it, don't buy it." That took guts and nerve, but it worked. By pleasing ourselves, we took everyone else on a magical mystery tour.

Hide the Wires—The popular belief is that everybody wants to know how the magic trick is done, but I disagree. I think we love to be fooled—to find out that someone is clever and resourceful enough to trick us even though we're so bloody smart. If you're attending a Katy Perry concert and she flies out over the audience during a song, you want to suspend your disbelief long enough so that for *just a second*, you believe she's really flying and not suspended by a harness.

When you're selling, the last thing you want to do is let the customer see the wires or the cards you have up your sleeve. Don't talk about your process for creating killer presentations. Don't explain how you found the buried fact that nobody else knew but that has your customer open-mouthed in surprise. Don't spill your secret for writing detailed proposals in half the time of your competitors. Let your results speak for themselves. Let the customer assume you're superhumanly gifted and be amazed.

DO YOUR HOMEWORK

You might not let on how you know all kinds of facts about your customer, his personal life, his company, and his market, but it's not magic. It's hard work. The first iPhone launched to acclaim and shouts of "Magic!" because the company shanghaied software engineers from all over the world to work eighteen-hour days and build its incredible, unprecedented user interface. Steve might not have cared about market research, but the engineers he imported knew what the state of the art in UI design was and brought that knowledge to the project.

Those intuitive, magical experiences where you seem to anticipate the user's needs before they have them and where you solve problems before they even exist? Yeah, they don't happen by accident. They happen because you do your homework, map out a long list of "If/Then" equations, and come to the table with your customer knowing more about him and his company than he does.

Research and intelligence-gathering is a superpower. Read everything you can get your hands on. Cultivate relationships throughout your industry, and never burn bridges. Map out hypothetical problems it would be valuable for you to learn about and solve, so if they come up, you're ten steps ahead of the customer. Learn about subjects that have nothing to do with selling to your market: music, literature, science, medicine, sports, history.

Because you're dealing with people, and people are motivated by curiosity and the desire to learn.

FEED YOUR BRAND

Imagine if you had a reputation as the best of the best: the sharpest, most ethical, most charming account executive at your company or in your industry. What would that do for your sales? It would be a like a proxy of you that arrived in your customer's office an hour before you did. The customer would be partially sold before you said a word.

Your reputation is your brand. It's similar to a musician on tour—what you're known for attracts fans and pre-sells tickets. So you should be guarding and growing your brand. Establish your values and don't deviate from them. Create materials that tell people who you are and what you stand for. Dress the part. Let people know about your achievements. Make sure your peers and customers know who you are and what you can do, and let your reputation speak for itself.

The Road to the Stage—Manager

You're ready. If you've absorbed everything I've shared, then you have the essentials to make magic. The most important thing you can do if you're leading a sales team is to guide your reps toward methods and approaches that they enjoy. Rote, lifeless selling will generate results just as lifeless. Variety, experimentation, personality—the more your people bring to the table, the more they'll like what they do, and their outcomes will reflect that.

The Road to the Stage—Individual Contributor

You're the musician downstage, in the spotlight. All eyes are on you. Relax. Seriously. When you're under stress, your recall goes south, and all that preparation and homework turns into a big blank space in your mind. So chill. If you've done the work, worked on your rhythm and words and harmony, if you've practiced listening and developed a great story, all you have to do is be yourself. You've got this.

You Can't See the Magic, So Take Delight in the Details

In 1988, I went from playing music for my supper to working in corporate America, and I got an ID for something called Apple Link, an email account that ran on the GE timeshare system. If you're not familiar with that, it means that email was processed on a shared mainframe computer that was probably the size of a Cadillac Escalade. Yes, times have changed.

Still, I had independence, and when I was handed the keys to my Pontiac company car, it was a station wagon. I went from semi-cool to mom-mobile. It took me a little while to get into the culture of rules—going somewhere every day, meeting with customers, making goals. What I found out was that I was fortunate to be in the education market, and even more fortunate to not be in K–12. Higher education was comfortable with my, er—*informal* persona. In other words, they liked that I was a smartass who cracked bad jokes all the time.

It took about a year and a half, and then one day it hit me: *I can do what these guys are doing.* My first goal was $800,000. I looked at that number and said "This is impossible. I'll never get to $800,000." I doubled it in that first year, and the euphoria from that never left me. It was my own standing ovation. Apple was a hard-driven sales organization, despite the talk of vision and magic. These things sell themselves? Bull. We worked hard and had sky-high expectations. "You're at two hundred percent of your goal? Great! What have you done for me lately?"

What I learned in those years was that I had to find my own standing ovations—we all did. You had to find the high and the rush in getting great results, working with terrific people, and solving problems, because:

Magic is invisible to the person making it.

When you're crushing a sales call, weaving a brilliant story, and taking the customer on an epic journey, you can't see it. You're in it. You can't see the trick any more than the magician making the card "appear from nowhere" can see the wonder. You're in on the trick. So you need to find other things to make you happy and keep you fired up. Is money one of them? Sure. But making people happy, the gratitude of a grateful customer, finding solutions for difficult problems, helping your company grow, savoring the independence of being on the road—those are all motivators than can fill your tank and make you better.

If you're creating that kind of joy and delight for yourself, that's how you know that the person in the audience is going to see magic. Great artists create for themselves, and hopefully their work finds an audience.

Michael's Excruciating Magic To-Do List:

- **Do the unexpected.** You don't want to bore the customer, but you shouldn't bore yourself either. Change things up from time to time: your rhythm, the cadence of your speech, your attire, whatever. Don't become too predictable, because that's the first step toward being taken for granted.

- **See magic shows and watch for the diversion.** Seriously, attend some magic shows. They're a blast. When you do, watch closely to see how the illusionist uses cognitive tricks to pull people's attention in one direction so he can make the quick moves that make the trick possible. For you, diversions are anything pleasurable that lower your customer's sales resistance: jokes, vacation stories, cool new gadgets, what have you. Figure out what your go-to diversions might be.

- **Develop your patter.** Magicians and musicians alike have patter—the casual-sounding stream of talk they use to warm up the audience and distract them from what they're doing. You should have patter as well, but for you it's the practiced order and cadence of your sales conversation: how you start your story, the transitions, the small details you throw in, the moment when you ask for the sale. If that's not refined and polished like a gold watch, you have work to do.

- **Destroy distractions.** When a concert venue or theater is too light, dark, hot, cold, crowded, smelly, smoky…it has the audience thinking about how uncomfortable they are, not about your performance. It wrecks the illusion and pulls people out of the magic. You won't always be able to dictate the location of your sales meetings, but if you can, do it. If you can't, try to take control of the lighting, temperature, and ambient sound. Turn off your phone, and see if you can get your customer to do the same for a few minutes. Do whatever you can to make everyone comfortable and have all their attention on you.

CHAPTER 10

A Painfully Obvious Musical Device: Seven Songs About the Future (Apple's and Yours)

"Do you want to spend the rest of your life selling sugared water, or do you want a chance to change the world?"

—Steve Jobs, persuading John Sculley to become Apple's CEO[9]

On March 25, 2019, Eddy Cue, Apple's senior vice president of Internet Software and Services, went public with something that Apple hadn't had in a while: an announcement of something new that many people thought was a terrible idea. The company would be rolling out Apple TV+, a new streaming service packed with original programming from artists like Reese Witherspoon, Oprah Winfrey, Steven Spielberg, M. Night Shyamalan, and so on. The move put Apple in the ring with experienced streaming fighters like Netflix, Amazon, and Hulu, and promises to further extend the Golden Age of Home Entertainment®.

---

9   John Sculley and John A. Byrne, *Odyssey: Pepsi to Apple: A Journey of Adventure, Ideas, and the Future* (New York: Harper Collins, 1987), p. 178

But Apple didn't stop there, and that's what I found interesting. The company also unveiled its own credit card—the Apple Card—which can be managed from your iPhone or carried in your wallet as a real, gorgeously designed (of course) sleek hunk of titanium. It's another example of what I said early in the book—of Apple's genius in creating things that you don't need but *want*, a status symbol that says, "Look, I'm in the tribe." As usual, the reviews for both were mixed. Apple TV+ was said to be a "me too" entry into a crowded streaming content world, and the Apple Card, while praised as a needed disruptor, also earned some scorn as another way for Cult of Mac members to run up debt.

I see that as a hopeful sign. Why? Because for years, Apple had a pattern:

1. *Announce a groundbreaking product that changes every-thing.*
2. *Be crucified in the press by people who insist the new thing is stupid, unnecessary, unworkable, etc.*
3. *Enjoy a colossal success.*
4. *Repeat.*

Think back to 2010, when Apple rolled out the iPad. Critics shredded it. They trashed it for being an oversized iPod Touch for old people. For not using Adobe Flash (Steve famously injured Flash with a single quip, and it never recovered). For being a front-end for iTunes. Even for having a name that sounded like a feminine hygiene product (stay mature, tech bloggers!). Even Steve was taken aback. Speaking to author Walter Isaacson for his biography, he said, "I got about eight hundred messages in the last twenty-four hours. Most of them are complaining… It knocks you back a bit."

The thing is, despite the derision, Steve and his team were right. The iPad was a blockbuster that created a new category and has changed how people consume media like movies and games. It's even changed education. When Apple rolls out something new and critics immediately attack it as impossible or impractical, that's usually a license to print money. Genuinely original, disruptive ideas are inherently risky. They're scary. They make people uncomfortable. And those are good things.

I've shared a lot about Apple's sales secrets and the music at their heart. I wish I could translate them into steps or a system, but learning to sell or build a sales operation like we had is more organic than that. It's about feel and pulse, not tools and workflows. So I want to conclude with my thoughts and advice about how you can take all this chatter about music, rhythm, words, and magic, and make it your own.

At the same time, since I started talking about writing this book, people have consistently asked me one question: "Where do you think Apple is going?" So I figured since I'm almost out of pages, I'd better give my adoring public what it wants and throw down a few predictions for Apple's future.

Now, here's where this all comes together. The values and character that made Apple an incredibly successful sales machine—and should continue to do so for the foreseeable future—are the same values and character that can make you successful. Your evolution and the company's evolution have a lot in common. So while I can't give you neatly packaged steps, I can predict what the future might look like and what you can do to get there. So let's do that.

And let's do it in song form, shall we?

1. "Imagine," John Lennon, 1971

I've talked off and on in these pages about the difference between leadership and management, and there's no clearer example of the distinction between the two than Steve Jobs versus current Apple CEO Tim Cook.

I'm not here to bash Tim; he stepped into an impossible role, succeeding a legend, and has steered the Apple ship with wisdom and care. But there's no denying the difference in the two men's styles. Steve was a *leader*, someone with a big, bold vision who challenged and inspired people to rise to the occasion—who shaped the times and the people around him. Leaders make us want to be better. They unsettle us. They motivate us to imagine the impossible. Steve did all those things.

Like many leaders, he could also be arrogant, callous, and uninterested in the human cost of his vision. That's where Tim came in. Tim is a *manager*. By and large, managers are not hubris-filled visionaries. They keep the trains running on time. They make sure the company is following the rules. They're the orderly *yin* to the leader's chaotic *yang*, and the greatest companies have both. When Apple was becoming Apple, we had both. Steve and Tim complemented each other perfectly.

But since Steve died, everyone has been waiting for that moment when Tim will step up and become Steve. That's not going to happen. That's not who he is. Everyone's waiting for Apple to announce its next "this changes everything" category buster, but I'm not sure there are any of those products left.

Think about the products that powered Apple's rise. Every one of them, with the exception of the iPad, was something that people already saw as a necessity. Millions were already carrying around music players. Practically everybody already had a mobile phone when the iPhone turned that category upside down. The Apple Watch…well, billions already wear watches. The iPad didn't follow this pattern, but it came along after the iPhone had already made people fall in love with touch screens.

There's not much of that low-hanging fruit left—maybe televisions, cars, and eyeglasses, but that's about it. That's why Apple TV+ and the Apple Card made sense. They're some of the last few holdouts. Unless someone comes up with something shockingly radical, we're already halfway out the exit from the Age of Breakthroughs. Like it or not, the future is going to be the Age of Iteration—of software, services, and incremental changes instead of giant leaps.

Steve was the perfect leader for an era of moonshots, for reinventing and creating categories. Does that mean Tim, with his focus on predictable improvement, efficiency and profitability, can't oversee breakthroughs? Certainly he can. Tim's a brilliant guy. But what made their collaboration work so well was that they complemented each other. There was always a vision of what Apple could be and what we could help our customers become, along with the skill to deliver. You'll need that balance, either in your individual sales career or if you're building a company. You need both imagination and efficiency.

Before Steve came back, I had to sell underpowered, immature products to colleges and universities. But while the devices hadn't caught up with the vision, the ideas were still there. Put control in the hands of the user, not the company. Make the mainframe and its network obsolete. They were philosophies, not selling propositions, and they spoke to people. They spoke to us. If you don't have a philosophy driving your selling, grow one.

At the same time, it's vital to understand that no matter how incredible software and services become, we'll never get away entirely from the good feeling of hardware, of something tangible. Adobe Creative Suite is as valuable to some of Apple's success as any device, but at the end of the day, you can't touch it. You can feel music, but it's different when you play it.

The future: Breakthroughs will become less common, but you will still need a breakthrough mentality that can help your customers feel wonder and excitement about what you're selling.

2. "The Thrill is Gone," B.B. King, 1969

Still, it's hard not to feel a little wistful about the old Apple. It's like Steve's death was literally the end of an era. It feels like all the geniuses are dead, and the joy of discovery is gone. That's depressing, because we crave wonder and magic. But they're not gone. They're just a little subtler, is all.

What people overlook is that Apple's success has never been about being first. We weren't the first with the MP3 player. We weren't the first with a personal computer with a mouse. We weren't the first with streaming. People misinterpret Apple's breakthroughs as firsts when they're really *functional* firsts. They're firsts that are great. They're firsts that are nuanced. Will Apple survive? Yes. Will it be the same company it was when I was there, when the device was everything and service was secondary? Probably not.

I think Apple will become a services company suited to the age of mobile apps, the cloud, and smart homes. Apple, Inc. will always make devices, but not quasi-magical devices that change the world. Instead, Apple's future objects will be platforms for delivering services that aren't limited by factors like rare earth metals and battery life. This goes right back to 1988, when our mission was to change the world one person at a time and build products to help individuals get things done. Tomorrow, it will be about perfecting the smart home, the smart office, the smart car, and creating immersive personal environments where everything responds to your command and even to your vital signs.

But that's still not enough for some people, and I understand if it's not enough for you. During the late '90s up to about 2010, Apple was Camelot. Once Camelot is gone, you can't recapture it. It was like the technology to create exceptional things came together in Cupertino with the vision and the will to get it done, and the result was enchanted. As I told you, I met the woman responsible for MP3 players with Sony at the ACE conference in D.C. At Sony back in 2000 and 2001, they had all the pieces, including the music library, to create something like the iPod, but they couldn't put it together. They lacked the vision and the will.

Breakthroughs are ephemeral. Magic fades. The pieces have to come together in just the right way at just the right time. Would the iPod have been as powerful without iTunes? No. Would iTunes have been possible without wireless broadband and then the cloud? No. Would digitization of music have happened if the MP3 format had remained part of the motion picture industry's protocol? No. Steve's gift, and what made Apple a breakthrough factory, was that we saw things coming together and acted.

That's gone. Mourn and then get to work. To borrow a line from *Avengers: Age of Ultron*, "A thing isn't beautiful because it lasts."[10] It's special because it can't be recaptured. Lovers of Apple need to accept that the era of Steve is gone forever, and that's okay.

As a sales professional, you can't always rely on enchantment either. It's terrific if you have a magical product to sell or you're madly in love with your work, but if that exultation is coming from something outside you, it's bound to fade. If you're dependent on that thrill to show up and do your job, what will you do when it's gone?

The solution is not to rely on something that's outside you but to find magic and music inside yourself. I had it because I loved everything about higher education and because I found the music in what I was doing—in weaving language into a story and feeling the rhythm of each encounter in a way that let the right thing happen at the right time. I'm a performer, and I loved performing live in sales as much as I loved performing live as a drummer.

The future: Dig deep, and figure out where the music is in what you're doing now. If you can't find it, you might have to go somewhere else until you do.

3. "Let's Work Together," Canned Heat, 1970

Apple's genius has always lay in taking complexity out of computing. In a meeting about the ease of use of a Mac, Steve said, "Computers are still too difficult to use." That was an amazing admission, because here was a guy who had made technology intuitive, made it work right out of the box, and had personally overseen the death of nerd-first command protocols like MS-DOS. (google that too.) But believe it or not, complexity in technology is still a problem for a lot of people. That's why Alexa and Siri are world-spanning spoken language interfaces and not just the names of Vegas strippers.

---

10   Feige, Kevin. *Avengers: Age of Ultron,* theatrical. Directed by Joss Whedon. Burbank: Walt Disney Studios Motion Pictures, 2015

Tim is more of a systems guy than Steve was, and that's perfect for the future. The next evolutions of Apple products will be in the *use* of the products, not the products themselves. In other words, how do they work for people and how do they interoperate with other technologies? There are still plenty of people who don't have Apple products. There's a lot of market to tap. Those markets will have different needs, different infrastructures, different challenges—and as the company strives to shrink the difference between iOS and the Macintosh, that will provoke some changes in how people can use things.

Let's look at a simple feature connecting the Mac and iOS: cut and paste between devices. If I copy something on my Mac in a word processing document, I can paste it across to my mobile device automatically through the cloud. If you take photos with your iPhone and you have your settings configured to save your photos to the cloud, they migrate there automatically. There's no barrier to interoperability between platforms.

Apple's biggest mistake would be to make the iPhone a Mac or the Mac an iPhone, because that's not what people want, but this tight integration builds a functional ecosystem. As we become more sophisticated in the way we write code and what machines can do, it's much more important how well things work together. As we head at full speed into edge computing, the Internet of Things, and decentralization of transactions, it's going to become more vital than ever that devices empower services that collaborate seamlessly.

Collaborating is just as critical for a sales professional. Too many of us are soloists, treating everyone else like rivals. At Apple, we were a unit, sharing ideas and approaches and keeping each other focused and positive. Be the one who figures out how, and your peers can work together to become a superior sales ecosystem. Open a dialogue. Create incentives. Explore everyone's strengths and weaknesses, and discover how you can make each other better.

The future: It won't be Willy Loman, the lone salesman on an isolated route. Sales, like everything else, will be crowdsourced and collaborative. The boundaries between the seller and the customer, once so clear, will begin to blur as middlemen disappear and transactions are direct and simple. Be on the forefront of that change.

4. "Don't Fear the Reaper," Blue Oyster Cult, 1976

I like my metaphors big and obvious...and with a great guitar lick. Here, the reaper isn't death but *failure*—the entrepreneur's death. That's what every company and executive fears...except Apple under Steve.

Here's a big problem that I see: too many people think being successful means being Steve and building their version of the Camelot-era Apple. But they can't, and not just because Camelot can't be recaptured (though that's part of it). When we were at our best, we were ten out of ten. That's transcendence, and getting there intentionally is like reaching the speed of light. I could assemble all the same people under one roof and not recreate it. It's something that just happens, and if you're lucky, it happens for a while. We were very lucky.

But most people don't understand what made Apple great. It's because we made things to please ourselves, not the marketplace. If you watch a lot of movies, you know that ninety-nine percent of the time, the sequel is worse than the original. That's true for music albums and books too. Why? It's because of a phenomenon I call *sequelitis*. When you're creating the first version of something, there's nothing at stake. There are no expectations, so you're free to create what delights you. You take risks, do crazy things, and work with passion. Sometimes, when you release what you've made into the wild, your daring originality strikes a chord with your audience, and they fall in love with what you've made.

Then, you get tapped to make a sequel. Now there are expectations. There's a rabid audience dissecting your film or TV show on *Reddit*. Fearing failure, you play it safe. Instead of doing something dangerous and original, you care what your audience thinks. In the end, you give them more of the same, instead of the electricity you gave them the first time around. The result is a bland, dull sequel. Very few artists—J.K. Rowling with *Harry Potter*; Joss Whedon with *Buffy the Vampire Slayer*—dodge this trap.

Apple created everything for Apple. We didn't give a damn what the market wanted; we would tell the market what it *needed*. We were creating for ourselves, and while we were doing that, education sales kept us alive, because academics are great about trying new stuff. Steve had no fear of failure, so neither did we. He considered his ideas to be a *fait accompli*. Eventually, the world would see that he was right, and that's usually what happened. But what makes his fearlessness important is that it's the one way you can "be like Steve."

Camelot might only happen when the stars align, but that doesn't mean you can't be a nine on a scale of ten with your own sales or your own company. You can be exceptional and do great things at that level. There's just one rule: you can't worry about failure either.

You're never going to be Steve Jobs. It's crazy to even try, because when you try to be Steve Jobs, you're not being you. Steve didn't try to be Bill Gates or Larry Ellison or Marc Andreessen. He was pure, unadulterated Steve. The only way you can find your own version of greatness as an individual salesperson or a company is to be pure, unadulterated you. That's the only part of Apple and Steve you should emulate. Stop caring what people think or what the market wants, and do what sets you on fire. If a brave idea flops, try another.

The future: You can copy what other people have done in their sales and pander to the market. That puts your chances of inspiring your customer at about...let's see...carry the three...*zero*. Or, you can be true to yourself, take risks, take the customer places he or she has never gone, and just maybe do the impossible. There are no guarantees, but you remain open to the possibility of music and magic.

Leaders don't worry about failure or making their own products obsolete. They want to do the unprecedented and leave people awestruck. In sales, you become a leader by not worrying about your numbers or even about closing the deal—at least, those goals are less important to you than making music and casting a spell that delights your customer. You take risks, try new things, make a human connection, and solve problems. In my experience, when you do that, sales take care of themselves.

5. "Let It Go," Idina Menzel, 2013

Yes, I'm citing something from the movie *Frozen*, which means the end times are right around the corner. But bear with me. In June of 2019, Tim Cook announced that Apple would end iTunes, breaking it up into Apple Music, Apple Podcasts, and Apple TV. I don't think most people realize what a watershed moment that was. It was Tim's first act of letting something go—of letting a once-beloved product die. Steve was spectacular at "killing his darlings," as the saying goes.

Let's face it: with streaming music, iTunes has become obsolete. But when it launched in 2001, it was a big deal. We had already been using it internally, because initially it was released on the Mac only, and then to Windows months later. Why? Because we had a test base of six hundred thousand rabid users who helped us work the bugs out before we went global. iTunes was Apple's first real venture into the Windows world, and it was the beginning of the idea of building a business around the platform, not the hardware. But what iTunes really represented was pure Apple: elegance and user interface perfection in a disjointed market.

Remember, Apple wasn't a company of firsts. We were a company of perfectly executed seconds. In other words, we took what other people had done poorly and made it work beautifully. Many others had tried to bring order to the music download fever of the 2000s, but Apple nailed it. iTunes brought organization, commerce, and structure to music. It made music personal. It gave everyone their own online record store. For me, it drove hardware sales from ones and twos to entire institutions, because in this new digital world, hardware was the connective tissue. But what nobody was willing to admit was that iTunes passed away with Steve Jobs. All Tim did was finally pull the plug.

The reason this is so important is that this was the first disruptive move of Tim's Apple. The first act of letting go of something everyone loved but that wasn't working anymore—an act at which Steve excelled. iTunes had become a kludgy Frankenstein's monster—a bolt here, a bolt there. Keep the trains running on time rather than creating a new mode of transportation. It became impossible to see the classic Apple perfection, focus, and user experience management in iTunes, so it was time for it to die. The death of iTunes is signaling Apple's rebirth under Tim in the same way the company was reborn when Steve came back and said to us, "We are more than computers. The iPhone is a phone, music player, and computer." iTunes is the most visible legacy of that Apple, and that Apple lives only in the past now—as it should be.

The future: Apple will now move to perfect the content distribution market, which will be a new focus for a media and hardware giant. The Mac will have to fully integrate into iOS. They will have to bring us new devices. The key is that this is the time for Tim to lead, not just manage. Apple unleashed creativity with iTunes and the App store while most people were looking for the newest flip-phone from Motorola. Steve, a master salesman, made that bold move possible. The next great sale is coming, this time from Tim's Apple. And if you think you know what's coming, you're probably wrong.

6. "Who Are You," The Who, 1978

I'm twenty-two years out from Apple, and I've gone through two or three other organizations. But after I decided I was tired of the startup world, I realized that I didn't have a good inventory of myself—of who I was and what I could do. I took a piece of paper, drew a line down the middle, and on the left side wrote who I thought I was. On the right side, I wrote who I want to be. And I limited myself to a single word, because words mean things.

I discovered that I wanted to be someone who influenced people. But I don't mean an Instagram influencer. Calling resorts and asking for free rooms because one hundred thousand people are bored enough to follow me on social media is a wee bit too high on the "look at me" meter for my taste.

I'm not an influencer in fashion or music. I make a mean glass of lemonade, but I'm not Beyoncé. But I've always been able to take people on a journey and see if I could help them. I like to keep things simple and direct. I like to educate people, to impart knowledge. I've seen what education does. It changes lives. That's why I've spent most of my adult life working in that world.

When I was done writing, on the left side of that page were terms like *discovery*, *partnership*, and *solution*—sales words. On the other side were words like *stewardship* and *solicitation*, and it occurred to me that those were a part of a world I thought I knew something about, which was fundraising for higher education. I figured I could transfer my skills to that world, do good, impact lives, and make a good living.

Well, it's sort of touching that I could be that naïve. I thought my skill would make fundraising a breeze, everyone would love me, and the marketplace would see the transferability of my value. Not so. The fundraising world had no clue. I had to teach them from the ground up how to value who I am and what I can do. They had a vocabulary, and I had to cross-reference. I've had depositions that were more fun.

The point is, whether you're an individual account executive or a leader building a sales organization, the world isn't obligated to value what you think it should. That's why focusing on sales mechanics and systems is a losing strategy. When we had a more traditional sales culture at Apple, focused on products and metrics, we sold less. Selling is about who you are. Apple gave me the ability and a leash long enough to learn who I was. They never gave me a prescriptive selling methodology. After Steve came back, we had sales leadership who didn't believe in individuals. They believed in groupthink. They didn't last long. We were offering to take people on a journey, and that doesn't fit into anybody's model.

We ditched off-the-shelf CRM solutions and spent the time and money to develop our own. Why? Because we were Apple. We didn't think like other companies, and we didn't act like other companies. We were collecting our data the way we wanted to. Why squeeze ourselves into their CRM like squeezing me into a pair of skinny jeans? (Sorry for that mental image.)

That tool led to a wonderful cross-pollination within our sales team. With each of us being ourselves, there on our CRM system for everyone else to see, we could see each person's strengths and creative ideas. We started feeding off one another. "What are you doing? How are you doing that?" It was collaborative and intense. We dropped "bought methodology" and ended up with a playbook based on our successes.

The future: If you're a sales manager or executive, this will be a challenge because you can't just implement a one-size-fits-all sales methodology across your organization. That's like trying to auto-tune every singer in a choir. What you end up with isn't music. So get the idea of some group sales culture out of your head. There isn't one. You're a conductor directing a bunch of individual artists, selling based on who they are. Respect for the individual melody should *become your culture*. That's where the joy and connection come from.

If you have a methodology, it will be the methodology of how each account executive approaches life. It isn't about selling; it's about who you are. That makes it easy to learn from each other and creates an atmosphere of openness and curiosity that's about selling but also about just getting better at being people. It's like a singer, drummer, and sax player each picking up tips and techniques from each other in rehearsal, instead of just learning from the "sage on the stage."

7. "Tangled Up in Blue," Bob Dylan, 1975

These days, everybody in business is trying to crack the code of Millennials and Generation Z. What do they want? How do we get them to buy? How can we convince them to stay in a job for more than a year? For the love of God, how can we kill the "man bun" for eternity? I'm a relatively old guy, so I don't have those answers. But I can tell you this with authority: millennials and Gen Z hate to be sold. Hate, hate, *hate*.

That's a problem, because they're the economic future. So stop selling. Start focusing on the journey and your common humanity. Talk and connect. Before Steve's return, Apple sales were all about the reporting. How much time did you spend during your call on the setup? Ten minutes? Okay. How did you set it up? What did you do? Did you close? We were cold and outcome-oriented, and it was miserable.

That will not work with the younger audience. If transactional selling isn't dead, then it's certainly out back coughing up blood. Selling can't be about the results anymore. Decoupling the process from the results is critical. I know, it's wrongheaded to sit here and say, "Don't look over the data." You're going to look at it. But it can't be the focus. Your focus should be the person you're calling on, the story you're telling, the journey you're taking the other person on, and the feelings you're evoking. It's like the best methodology is no methodology. It's just people.

If you want to see that in action, visit an Apple Store. They have metrics. But it's all about taking the customer on a journey. If that takes an hour, it takes an hour. It's healthy and human and welcoming. And it works. There isn't another retail experience like it. In the Apple Store, no one is trying to sell you, and it's obvious. They're trying to connect with who you are and what you need. It's selling by not selling.

That was Apple. Many times I walked into an Apple Store and handed someone my business card, and they had no idea the direct sales force even existed. We were the largest sales team you never heard of, because we didn't sell.

The future: That's why I chose *Tangled Up in Blue* here, one of the great storytelling songs in the American folk canon. Everything is becoming about personalization and authentic human storytelling. The coercive sell is basically dead; someone just needs to drive a stake through its heart and cut off its head so it can't rise like Christopher Lee in those Hammer *Dracula* films.

We live in a personalized economy now. You have your own personal taxi service with Uber and Lyft. You have your own personal hotel chain with Airbnb. You have your own personal retail store called Amazon that brings you anything you want. You have an agent called Alexa, and your wish is her literal command.

You can't fight this current. Don't even try. You are swimming upstream when you say, "We're going to shove you into the same mold as everyone else." Not anymore, you're not. You'll drown. Everything is real and personal and built around authentic storytelling and caring. Anything less and you may as well find a new profession.

8. "Pride and Joy," Stevie Ray Vaughan, 1983

When I was doing interviews in the startup world, I would see people's *LinkedIn* pages, and they would just be lists of one-word skills. Negotiating. Sales. Marketing. That's nothing. Those are sockets in a socket set. I don't care what you know. I didn't make it twenty-two years because I knew every inch of every Apple product. I care about who you are.

If I could give managers one piece of advice, it would be to *stop being coaches*. You're not here to coach. You're here to create harmony. You're here for individuals. You're here to create a safe space for people to express their artistry.

Automation is replacing sales in some areas, but real person-to-person sales will never disappear, because to be human is to sell. Selling isn't just a transaction concerning a product, a price, and a deliverable anymore. True sales never was. Sales is us persuading someone to see our point of view, give us a chance, accept our invitation; hire us. You might lead a team that's birthing ideas and wants to create a market. That's selling.

All salespeople are artists in some way. Sales is the ultimate nuanced profession, though no one recognizes that. At its heart, it's about relationships and understanding people, bringing them to a time and place where they believe that anything is possible.

The Ace Hotels chain is a great example. The guy who created it, the late Alex Calderwood, was a little nuts. But he was also creative and intense and fearless. He was an artist, and he created an experience. He reinvented the experience of being in a hotel—made it communal and bespoke with a kind of hipster, speakeasy feeling. Was he selling? Absolutely. But it wasn't Marriott. It wasn't Hilton. Airbnb is killing them. It was personal.

Apple had a three hundred-person sales force, but we never sold anything. We were agents of ideas. We were bringing people into the fold and taking them somewhere. Yes, there was a product, a price, and a deliverable. But that wasn't the focus. We had a bigger mission.

The future: Do you know what your mission is? It can't be to hit your numbers, or you're done before you start. If you're in the medical world, can your mission be to sell more surgical robots? No. *Your mission must be something that you care about personally.* That's what will separate you from the order-takers. Maybe your mission is to improve healthcare, make doctors' lives easier, or make surgery affordable to people in poor countries. Those are purposeful ideas. Those are missions.

Sales has become about heart. In a nutshell:

Sales is not selling.

That's a brain-busting Buddhist koan for you, courtesy of a drummer who still loves disco. But if you're leading a sales force, and you can make them conscious of the truth—selling is the last thing they are doing—they will be much more effective. So will you.

We all want to be creative. We all want to be artists. No kid says, "I want to be an order-taker when I grow up." If you want a future in sales, find your music. Find what lights you up and makes you approach your work with pride and joy. I'll never forget a shoe shine guy I had who was like that. I was staying at the Gaylord Hotel in Washington, D.C., and this gentleman who shined my shoes was an amazing individual. Not because what he was doing was changing the world, but because of the music and heart he brought to it. He put two kids through college shining shoes, and he's an inspiration to me to this day.

It's easy to be exalted by work that everyone tells you is important or influential or difficult. But that's about your ego. Finding pride and joy in humble, small things—like giving someone a perfect shoe shine or making a college provost grin when he sees how easy it was to get your computer on his network—takes character and self-awareness.

On Side B of the *Apple Boogie* cassette is a song titled "The Apple II Forever." Well, nothing is forever. Musical styles come and go. Your mission isn't a number. It's not a deal. It's finding your music and bringing it to the people you sit down with. If you can do that, the rest is easy. So go do it.